CALLED TO THE ARCTIC: THE MEMOIRS OF REV. MIKE GARDENER

Michael George Gardener

ISBN-13: 9798648059122
ISBN-10: 1477123456

Cover design by: Michael Gardener
Library of Congress Control Number: 2018675309
Printed in the United States of America

For all the past and present people of Nunavut and elsewhere who are pictured or written about in this book and have helped and supported us so much.

CONTENTS

Title Page   1

Copyright   2

Dedication   3

EDITOR'S PREFACE   7

Introductions   15

Chapter 1: EARLY DAYS   17

Chapter 2: THE FIRST POSTING—LAKE HARBOUR   33
(KIMMIRUT)

Chapter 3: KINNGAIT   122

Chapter 4: PANGNIRTUNG AND THE ARTHUR TURNER   157
TRAINING SCHOOL

Chapter 5: OUR IQALUIT LIFE   171

Chapter 6: RETIREMENT   190

Concluding remarks   201

EDITOR'S PREFACE

A warning, dear readers: you are about to embark on an adventure with a pair of intrepid souls who were willing to experience life in the Arctic when the word "remote" really meant something. Prepare yourself to read about homes without plumbing, communication by parachute mail drop, travel by dog team… and about how life has changed dramatically for Inuit over the course of the last 50 or 60 years. In his stories, Mike Gardener describes his personal journey in serving God in the Canadian Arctic, accompanied by his beloved wife Margaret. And, like the Inuit to whom he ministered, he isn't shy about describing life in all its down-to-earth details.

When I was approached by Mike's family to see if I would be willing to edit his memoirs, how could I say no? I am indeed an editor by profession, and spent over 25 years working in the part of Canada now called Nunavut. But more importantly, for many years I was one of Mike's parishioners in Iqaluit, and was privileged to experience first-hand the degree of love and care he exercised as a pastor over his flock, and the loving support provided by Margaret in this ministry. When I was a newly arrived young mother in Iqaluit in 1985, my sanity was saved by Margaret's "Moms and Tots" program. Then, for many years, my contribution to St. Jude's Cathedral parish life was to direct the choir for the English-speaking congregation, and weekly Mike and I would discuss the service's lessons to choose the most appropriate hymns. I have vivid memories of his penchant for illustrating sermons not only with the famous Andy Capp cartoons, but with physical demonstrations to bring theological points to life—such as using a boiling kettle (steam), a glass of water and some ice cubes to illustrate how God can, like water, be three different things but still the same One. Although I fear my brother-in-law was almost too terrified to return, when on attending his first service there, he was nearly beaned by the kite Mike attempted to fly across the front of the nave in order to illustrate the lifting power of the Holy Spirit.

On a more serious note, you will hear in reading these memoirs Mike's very humble and self-deprecating voice, describing the many adventures experienced by him and Margaret in ministering to the Inuit of South Baffin Island. His commitment to learning and preaching in Inuktitut, and in experiencing and absorbing traditional Inuit life in the small communities and outpost camps, gave him real insight into the needs of his parishioners, and, very importantly, an unparalleled ability to understand the worldviews of Inuit, especially those called into the service of Christ in many forms. Many of Mike's theological students have gone on to form the backbone of the current Inuit clergy in the Anglican Church in Canada and become key translators of the full Bible into Inuktitut, from the foundation of their Bible studies together. He is very modest about that accomplishment.

In these days when "reconciliation" is a buzzword in Canadian society's relationship with Indigenous peoples, Mike and Margaret's life together was a true exemplar of those who would reconcile people with God, and with each other. Both of them ministered in their own ways to everyone around them, but the bottom line was always that if someone needed care, counselling, or ministry, they could count on the Gardeners for support.

I hope you enjoy and are uplifted by reading Mike's recollections.

EDITOR'S NOTE: INUKTITUT USAGE
Mike Gardener's mission to the Inuit of the Eastern Arctic has largely been conducted in Inuktitut, particularly those dialects

spoken on Baffin Island. Since the late 1900s, this language has primarily been recorded in writing through the use of "Canadian Aboriginal Syllabics," as they are defined in the international Unicode standard. On the subject of using syllabics, Mike says:

Syllabics were originally developed by James Evans, a missionary to the Cree in the mid-1800s, as they had no written language. The system that he invented was based on shorthand and listening very carefully to the phonetic sounds the Cree Indians spoke.

This system was adopted by the first missionary to the Eastern Arctic, Rev. Edmund Peck, in the 1870s. He used the Greenlandic texts of the New Testament already translated from German into roman orthography, but changing a lot of the words into Eastern Arctic Inuktitut dialect, and also using syllabics based on the Cree Indians' system, to shorten the many long words when written out in roman orthography. So Rev. Peck set about producing copies of the New Testament Gospels, adding a few prayers, a few hymns and basic instruction on the Christian Faith, to distribute these to the Inuit in the Eastern Arctic. These were the basic materials used to spread the Gospel even without a resident missionary in each camp. Inuit leaders were trained to do this by Peck.

Syllabic scriptures and prayer books were therefore used widely, as Inuit themselves generally found syllabics easy to learn and use, leading to widespread literacy, particularly among church-going Inuit.

Several different forms of "roman orthography" have been developed over the years to express Inuktitut words in the standard alphabet used by most European languages, to make them easier to read for people who do not know syllabics. However, Mike's own preference is to spell Inuktitut in syllabics. Speaking from my own experience, he was known as a very creative (that is to say, non-standard) transliterator of Inuktitut into roman, in his days in Iqaluit ministering to both Inuktitut and English-speaking congregations. So with his permission, many of his personal transliterations of Inuktitut words in his original manuscript have been standardized to the orthography used by the Government of Nunavut for the purposes of this book. We have chosen in a few instances to include the syllabic representation of an Inuktitut word first, so that readers can see and understand the world Mike worked in, but generally roman orthography will be used for Inuktitut terms, which will be explained or defined when they are first used.

Many Inuit personal names dating from the early days of Mike's ministry were also expressed in what would now be considered "non-standard" roman orthography for the purposes of administration (church, government and health records, for example). These forms have been retained, as they were the spellings used by the individuals in question.

All Inuktitut place names will be given their current accepted roman orthography spelling, in accordance with Government of Nunavut standard usage (corresponding with current maps of Nunavut).

Where a community had an English name for a while, and has now reverted to and officially adopted its Inuktitut name, as in the case of Frobisher Bay/Iqaluit or Lake Harbour/Kimmirut, the English name will be retained when it is a representation in the text of the historic period or something being said at the time. For example, Mike's original mission mandate was to "Lake Harbour" and it was referred to as such in the correspondence of the day. Generally, however, the current name of the community will be used in referring to it.

Interestingly, while the manuscript was in the course of being edited, the Nunavut communities of Cape Dorset and Hall Beach officially adopted changes back to their Inuktitut names, during the 2020 Winter Sitting of the Nunavut Legislative Assembly. They are now known as Kinngait and Sanirajak, respectively. Mike prefers to refer to Cape Dorset as Kinngait, so the same naming principles have been applied for it as well.

Carol Rigby, Editor

Margaret and the author, Mike Gardener in an undated
photo. Photo credit: Scott Wight Photography.

INTRODUCTIONS

Hello, my name is Michael Gardener—most people call me Mike. My mother was called May Eleanor, maiden name King, and my father was George Edwin Gardener. I was born in New Malden, Surrey in 1930. I lived there for about five or six years.

My Mum and Dad

My wife Margaret was born in a small hamlet, Frith Common, near Tenbury Wells in Worcestershire. She entered this world in May 1929. Later on I will talk about our life together as Rev. and Mrs. M. Gardener!

Margaret's Dad with his daughter and a friend (Molly)

I dedicate this book to my wife, Margaret, three daughters, foster son, nine grandchildren, 16 great-grandchildren (so far!) and one great-great-grandchild (also so far!), and to all our friends, both Inuit and non-Inuit, who have helped us in our journey together in our Christian life, to make our time in the Arctic possible. I have tried to write this autobiography as close as possible to the events that actually occurred, even if to some readers these events might seem to be rather too much "down to earth."

CHAPTER 1:
EARLY DAYS

"Michael, what have you done?" my mother said as she looked at me all covered with soot. I had only been "painting" the garden path with a nice mixture of soot and water! The soot was from a pile somewhere in the garden that my father used to put around his plants to improve the soil. I was promptly put in a bath and washed clean. It was easier for me to be cleaned than the garden path! Another time, while my mother was in hospital for a procedure, I must have got bored while I was left to amuse myself. I had a book of cartoons for kids. I tore out one page at a time and went around delivering each page to all the neighbours' letter boxes. Another time I went shopping with my mother. I was on a little tricycle that had no brakes on it. I just freewheeled down the hill near our home at a great pace on the sidewalk, almost knocking people over! I guess I was a bit wild and adventurous from a very early age. Also I believe I was toughened up by my mother from my earliest years, being left outside in my pram in winter, in spite of all the neighbours complaining that I would "catch my death of cold."

My mother was a very kind, caring person, and I owe so much to her for my upbringing and later life. She also made sure I said my prayers at night! In those days fathers seemed much more distant from their children than today, and so I do not really have any special recollections about my Dad. I only know he worked for the Southern Railway Co. as a salesman to get people to send their supplies by rail, rather than by road. In those days there were no TVs, Lego™, video games and so on to amuse us, but we found our enjoyment in taking the dog for a walk, playing on the swings in the park, going to the store, watching the ants on the sidewalk, playing with toys that wound up, and so on. I do not remember my mother ever getting mad with me – such was her patience.

When I was about five or six years old, my father got worried about his mother who lived in Egham, Surrey. She lived in a house called Woolston, and he felt he should be there with his mother because she was blind with glaucoma. I do not know if she had any other problem besides being blind. So my father got us moved there. I think he did this rather much against my mother's wishes, because my mother and his mother did not get along well together – justifiably! My grandmother was a very hard person to get along with. I was mean to her. When she was angry over something and retreated to her room, and was about to slam the door, after calling me a "dirty rat," I would quickly slip a mat into the doorway so that she couldn't close the door – I don't know what she called me then! That is my recollection of her. My father was very protective of his blind mother and she of him – for example, when we had the main meal together, I would announce in my "innocent voice" for my blind Granma to hear: "Mum has finished first." Granma would reply: "She's a quick eater!" If I announced that my Dad finished first she'd say: "Poor boy! He didn't have much to eat!" This over-protectiveness eventually led to my parents having to split up.

Whilst there, living at Woolston, I went to a little school nearby, about a hundred yards away. It was a happy time at school. There I learned the usual things, especially mental arithmetic, which I found very useful later on in life. They drilled multiplication tables into you and gave a prize of sixpence for those who did best at it – I won only once.

The day war broke out, September the 3rd 1939, I can picture us in the living room hearing this news, as we gathered around the radio -- I was waiting for the bombs to drop right away! Of course none came. The air raid siren went, but no bombs, no planes. We waited and waited and nothing happened. Then, more or less the next week or two after war broke out, my mother couldn't take it anymore. She decided to go out with me and search for other accommodation. I can remember trying to find some in the next town called Staines, but no luck. She finally found a place in the main High Street of Egham above a food store. It was very handy because rationing was going to start, and being above the food store, you'd get a few extra bonuses from the ration amount. I can remember it was a ration of two ounces of butter, two ounces of tea and four ounces of sugar a week. Even bread became more or less rationed as well, let alone candy, chocolate bars, eggs, clothing, meat, etc. There was no such thing as fresh fruit, only what was locally grown.

As the war advanced, in the early '40s, more German raiders started coming. My father was still living at Woolston with his mother. He was worried about us and he arranged for a shelter to be built in our backyard garden in the High Street – a small garden it was, but there was room for a concrete shelter. He also arranged for steps to be built from my bedroom down into the back garden or backyard so that when the air raid siren went, I could go down those steps with my mother and go into the newly-built shelter.

In the meantime there was my other grandmother, my mother's mother. She was evacuated from Caledonian Road in North London, where she had an apartment. It was too dangerous to live there because of all the bombs being dropped in that area, so she chose to stay with us. I was very happy. I loved my second grandmother. She used to tell me made-up stories I can more or less still remember, about tramp (Hobo) number one, tramp number two three and four, and their adventures and how they were given blankets to keep them warm. When the air raid siren went, she would go along with my mother and me, down the newly constructed steps, into the shelter in our garden. There we would "camp," usually for the whole long night.

The bombs would be dropping quite close to us at times. In fact, one night there was a terrific explosion and it was a bomb just about two hundred metres away from us. Two stores in the High Street had received a direct hit by an incendiary bomb, and were completely destroyed. One person was killed and two injured in that explosion. You can see the damage below:

Two stores that were bombed close to our home.

That was quite a shock to us all. I believe all the glass from the storefront below our flat blew out as well, from the blast. But we were safe in our little concrete shelter! When we were in it, I would have been laid out on the concrete floor with a bit of padding underneath my blankets. My grandmother and my mother each had a deck chair to sleep in. We had a candle in an earthenware pot with an upturned earthenware pot over it. This gave us a little light and even a bit of heat. We were not allowed to have any exposed light, because that would be a sign for where the Germans could drop their bombs. We stayed in that shelter all night, even after the "All Clear" had sounded. Then we went to breakfast and to school later. That is the sort of life we had!

My "Agreement with God"

I went to a different school when I got to be 10-years-old. It was a secondary school called Strodes, which was fairly near our flat. There we also could shelter from the air raids. When the warning siren went, we were quite happy, because that meant that we could skip class and go down to the shelter underneath the school. We kids had a good time there in the shelter. We played Battleships, Hangman's Noose, Tic-tac-toe and other games. As we played these games we had jam sandwiches with reconstituted orange juice. That was our snack whilst we waited for the "All Clear" to go – we did not go home until it sounded.

It was in this school, Strodes, that I made a real turning point in my life. In those days even Government schools had a Morning Assembly –not just singing "God Save the King," but also a short Scripture reading, hymns, prayer and a talk, nearly always given by the school principal. His name was Captain Gittings. One morning he gave a talk on David Livingstone as a missionary going to Africa. Somehow or other, that talk he gave hit right home to me. I was just 12-years-old. I said in my mind, "Okay God, let me go to be a missionary, but don't send me where it's hot. I'll go where it's cold!" In those days, and maybe still today, I didn't like being in a place that's too hot or enclosed. I didn't like the heat of some of the summers then, let alone now in Ottawa! That's why I said to God, "Send me to where it's not hot. I'll go where it's cold." And I sort of added in my mind, "Well God, You will like me if I can become a missionary, and I can maybe go to heaven." Something like that I thought in my boyish mind, not really fully understanding the real Gospel message.

To this day it makes me think how God works in many ways. God is so patient with us! He starts working in us by His Spirit in various ways, even if we misunderstand them at the time. Then there comes a time when we finally come to accept Him into our lives. For some His prompting can be like what happened to St. Paul on the road to Damascus; to others it can be a slower realisation of our need of a Saviour. He is always there, leading us to Him – no one is beyond hope! God has timing that He knows the best, not our timing. I believe that God used my mother's loving upbringing of me, and even being left outside in my pram in winter, as means to a future calling to the Arctic. God always sends us for His work to be done whenever and wherever possible!

In spite of my "agreement with God," even for a while after, like many boys growing up, I was sort of wild – swearing, smoking cigarettes with my friends, going with the crowd, going to the River Thames, sunbathing every day, getting red-skinned and then darkish brown skinned – no lotion – not afraid to lie out in the sun more or less all day, wading in mud up to my knees, gulping down some "good" River Thames water as I was swimming. We played around throwing mud at each other – we had a great time! I do believe that surviving dirty water and the mud lets you have an immunization for the future. Children are too "clean" now, to later on benefit from immunisation to dirt in their lives.

When I come to think of it, we didn't really take much notice of the war, not in the earlier days, but we were blessed and very fortunate, as nothing terrible happened to us.

Doing these activities as a kid, as well as going biking and "exploring" places, I hardly ever went to church. On a Sunday morning, instead, I had to go and see my father who was still at Woolston, and do something with him. He'd get me to dig the garden a bit, or something like that, then I'd go back to our flat, all muddy and sort of yucky. My mother would have a bath ready for me and I'd go straight into the bath, midday, on a Sunday. My father definitely was not a churchgoer then! However, later on as my parents got older, that changed. My mother started to go to our local Church of England. I'd go to Church with my mother and that woke me up spiritually, to start to realise that I needed a cleaner lifestyle and to get right before God. Later on, my father started to go to church in Staines, a town near to Egham. He was shy about going to the local church, where he would be more known, so my parents would both walk to Staines and I'd join them after I biked there. The minister was the Reverend Cecil Sharpe, a very stern, foreboding type of man. So I didn't really like going there. I preferred going to our local Egham church, which was friendlier and less formal!

When I was nearly 15 years old, my father thought I should go to a different school from Strodes. Maybe he thought that I'd be getting into bad company if I stayed there. Oddly enough, the school that he proposed I go to, Beaumont College, was a Roman Catholic school. It was a boarding school, although I went as a day boy – I hated it! The Jesuit teachers were so solemn and out of touch. It also seemed to be in such a grim setting, and most of the kids were so "upper class" and cliquish. I didn't go home for lunch, although this school was only about a 20-minute bus ride from home. The school had to feed us lunch. There were only a very few of us who were day boys. No girls there! We would sit around a refectory-type table and be portioned out food by a head boy. The allowance was one paper-thin bit of roast beef, one potato and one spoon full of vegetables. That was starvation for growing guys! In the late afternoon I would go home and my mother, bless her, would've cooked up something for me, so I could fill up on that. I bet I was really eating up a good part of her food ration as well as mine!

After this Beaumont College experience, I persuaded my parents (I don't remember if it was my mother or father or both) that I should leave school. I left after Junior Matriculation – that'd be after Grade 9 in Canada. I'd had enough of school. By the way, I never went to Sunday School as a child, because I said, "I go to school in the week. I don't want to go to Sunday School as well, as I have had enough of school in the week!" That was a silly thing I said. After I left Beaumont College, my father tried to get me work, to make myself more useful. He did find a place for me, working in a market garden. There I worked from 8 a.m. to 6 p.m., but went home by bike to our flat in the High Street for lunch. I helped grow tomatoes, pinch out chrysanthemum side shoots to make them have larger and better blooms, and get rid of earwigs in the earwig traps that were put on the pole above the chrysanthemum or dahlia plants. The owners of the market garden also had about 12 heifers. An old guy, Ben, and myself had to feed them, and put fresh straw down in their pound. I thought it a treat to go in and throw mangelwurzels (a type of large beet used as cattle fodder) to them. I was wary of the beasts but never felt scared.

While working there and having got more involved with things at my home church I started to do a little bit of church work, teaching Sunday school. Aha! That was funny, having never been to Sunday school myself! There was a very kind minister named John Northridge in charge of Egham Church. He's dead now, but he encouraged me a lot. He started a young peoples' group called the Anglican Young People's Association (AYPA). Fancy name for a youth group! I don't think they were all that young either! I'm sure there were quite a few older than me, but it was a group that I enjoyed. Also, Rev. Northridge got me helping with the Boy Scouts Cub Pack in addition to teaching the Sunday school. I even went to a weekend training camp for Cub leaders. We got ideas for games and things that would become useful for the future.

Although the war had finished in 1945, there was still conscription going on by the British government. All those 18 and over would be called up for an 18-month period in the Forces, whether you liked it or not. But there was an exception! Those working on the land would not be called up. I think, at this time, my parents were really wondering what I was going to do. Would I make market gardening my career, or what else? I think at that time I wondered whether I should sign up to be a train driver or a chef or something like that. Should I really be thinking of the "cold Arctic"?? However, deep down I felt convinced that I was called to go there as a missionary. My parents did not know this, as I was too shy to tell them, although I eventually had to break the news. This deep conviction that I had to go to the Arctic, even if it didn't seem to make sense, made me realise that I couldn't just "mark time" in the market garden, but had to get on and do what I had to do. I would have to leave the market garden and thus be conscripted.

We had a choice of military services, and I chose the Royal Air Force (RAF). Then we had to choose three "careers" we'd like to pursue, and would hope to get our first choice. My first choice was to be a Nursing Orderly. I thought it might be useful for the future. I got it! However, you first had to do "square bashing" before the Nursing Orderly training began. This six-week course was held at Bridgenorth in the Midlands. It was quite a challenge to me to be away from home for the first time and for such a long period. I felt weird and lost! I did not do very well in square-bashing, with all of its drill and rifle positions and everything else. When the square-bashing, six-week training period was over, our platoon had a passing-out parade, with us trying to beat other platoons. I guess my Platoon Leader was embarrassed by my lack of coordination and my odd way of marching with my prominent seat. He said, "You better go instead and do canteen duty!" In other words, he'd get me out of the way so I wouldn't embarrass the rest of the platoon!

I left Bridgenorth and was given 48 hours leave to go home before going for my training to be a Nursing Orderly, to a place called Moreton-in-the-Marsh in Gloucestershire. I really enjoyed that training about basic First Aid, and a bit about medicine and splints, and all that sort of thing.

After the training had finished in Moreton-in-the-Marsh, I was sent to a small place called Hockering in Norfolk. There was I – weirdly enough – the only medical person in the whole place, responsible for a hundred servicemen. I really prayed that there would not be a bad accident! Me in charge of that sort of thing! On the whole it was all very quiet without incident. People just came in with coughs and colds and I gave them their Aspirin, cough medicine, "Mist Expect Stim" and other medications. I also had to look after the Blue Room (a place to control STDs). I was posted to Hockering for over a year. I would sometimes try and hitchhike home – various people would give me a ride to the subway in the east part of London. That would connect me with a train to get to Egham. There I'd go for a 48-hour pass. Somehow or other I managed it. In those days there was no big issue about not picking up people trying to hitchhike, so I was very blessed to meet the right people going to the right place.

University and Theological College
It was because I went into the Air Force that I was able, after being demobilized, to get into university without having to have Senior Matriculation (Grade 12 graduation). My Junior Matriculation was sufficient and that was a blessing. Then I had to choose subjects to do after the Air Force.

I demobbed around June 1950, and then I was more or less free. I did a vacation job to earn a bit of money before going to university. I had to go around as a salesperson, selling these special tickets with which stores would mark their items for sale. I got a commission for doing this. The tickets were really very shoddy, but I managed to sell quite a few of them. That was all practice for passing on information to people, or getting used to being with people I didn't know. I'm naturally very shy and it was very hard for me to do that then. In school or elsewhere I would never get up in front of people. I'd avoid it like the plague! One time the minister at Egham asked me to read a Bible reading at an evening service in the Church there. He gave me two weeks warning. I got more nervous as the day got closer. I kept on imagining myself going up in front of those 150 or so people. I did manage though, after much encouragement from my mother!

I also got part-time jobs as a collector of dirty dishes in the Waterloo Station Cafe. Other jobs I did were rolling out and cutting out denim jeans, metalwork (putting metal off-cuts, called swarfs, into an extractor that spun around, to collect the oil on them) and delivering newspapers.

It was whilst I was in the Air Force that people called "Scripture Readers" came and got me thinking about who or what is a Christian. Until that time, I just thought that you had to obey the Ten Commandments and have something doing that's pleasing to God before you might possibly be accepted by God. In other words, I thought then that we have to make all our own effort to try and earn our way into heaven. We know now that we're not saved by what we can do, because nothing can ever be good enough to save us just by our own efforts. We know that Jesus is the only answer. It's a finished fact of His dying for us on the cross and rising from the dead. It is His sacrifice on the cross that saves us alone. It is also a continuing personal relationship with Him that we must have, after we have accepted Him into our hearts and lives. We know He accepts us just as we are, even with all our weaknesses and faults Somehow, this Scripture Reader person got that message over to me. The Lord used him and I realized that if I went to Africa, wherever I went to, it wouldn't make any difference. It is because as Ephesians says, "By grace we are saved." In other words, we are saved by God's love, which we don't deserve – you and I are saved to be with God here on Earth and for eternity. It's only accepting that fact that makes us want to lead a life here on Earth that is inspired and enabled by God's love. Yes! Even me!

It is God's love that gets into our hearts, that saves us for eternity.

It was while I was in the RAF that I had written to the then Bishop of the Arctic, Archibald Fleming, about my wish to serve in the Arctic. He was very welcoming to me regarding my request. Here is one of his letters of encouragement that he wrote to me in reply to my letter to him:

21st June, 1949.

2425033, A/C2 Gardener
898 Course,
Training Squadron,
MTG and D
Moreton-in-Marsh, Gloucester, England.

My dear young Friend:

I was delighted to receive your letter dated 28th May and to hear all your interesting news. It is quite evident that you are having all kinds of new experiences and changing around from place to place has its advantages.

I note with pleasure your program of studies and also that you are acting as Server in the Chapel. All this will prove invaluable to you in the future and remember that there is no experience so helpful as personal contacts with men of all kinds - good, bad or indifferent. My experience has taught me that to be an effective minister of the Gospel you must first love God and then love your fellowmen and you cannot expect that your fellowmen are all going to have the same standards and ideals that you have. It is by friendly, kindly intercourse but standing resolutely for those things which are good and pure and true that you will influence others so that they will be lead into the obedience which our Saviour requires.

With prayerful good wishes for your every blessing,

Yours very sincerely,

28

After leaving the Air Force in 1950, I went to Reading University. I enjoyed my time there. I had to choose my subjects, and I chose to study English, French, and Psychology. My thinking was that I'm not much good at school subjects, although I had to put up with two of them as required subjects for my BA course. I thought that I would have a better chance in majoring in a non-school subject – Psychology. Also I hoped that this subject would be helpful for me in my future work. So that is what I did.

There were disastrous results from my first English and French exams! I was horrible at languages. I had to study Latin at Beaumont College and I really hated it, even with the extra tuition in the subject that my Dad had arranged. There were Latin's masculine, feminine, neuter, different types of endings, irregular verbs etc., and same with French! Well, there's no neuter in French but it's still a problem "Is that a man or a woman?" Well, is a pen masculine or feminine? – that sort of thing. So I didn't do well at all, but I was given a second chance – I would sit the same exam again. That was divinely arranged, I am sure! I did do very well in my Psychology exam the first time. So then the next time, my second chance, I concentrated much more on the French and the English. I was told I did very well in them, but not very well at Psychology. Obviously that's a rebound effect and they understood that, thank goodness. I was there at Reading University for three years, going home by train from Reading every day. I also joined the University Yacht Club, as I thought it might be handy practice for sailing in Arctic boats, which I thought would also be sailing vessels. Little did I know the real facts!

I could not keep my choice of going to the Arctic secret any longer from my parents, so with some shyness I had to finally tell them. My father did not like the idea and thought I was really crazy. "You'll freeze to death," he said. My mother, bless her, tried to make the best of it and encouraged me to proceed. So with her acceptance of what I wanted to do and the Bishop's letter, these really were encouragements and confirmation of what I felt called to do. To me it confirmed that this calling was from the Lord.

I still got a lot of pressure from my father not to waste my time by going to the Arctic, when I did so well in Psychology. I did very well because I thought the many facets of Psychology were all interesting and necessary. They would help me in my future ministry, working with people. A big bonus was that we didn't have any exams at all for nearly two and a half years! However, we had to do our thesis in that time, and I did mine on "frustration." I had to go down into the basement of the university and frustrate people there. What did I do to achieve this "wicked" goal?? First of all I would give them some easy motor skill game, which required the person to hit targets on a revolving drum. Then I asked them easy questions, and they'd answer these correctly – but I'd tell them it was the wrong answer! Then I'd repeat the skill game again and see how the scores were significantly different from before the frustrating experience. I enjoyed myself doing that! Cruel!! After about 12 unlucky subjects had finished my experiment, I would work it out with various logarithmic tables as to how much does a frustrating experience affect a person's work habits and motor skills? Of course it came out as a positive result, statistically significant. We had great teachers there at the University and I had a great time.

After my three years at Reading University, I had to go more or less straight away to theological college. I did not want to go to some very stiff and starchy college. I wanted to go to one more down-to-earth and Evangelical. I chose, oddly enough, one that was in Oxford. It turned out, although it was in Oxford City itself, it had not anything directly to do with the University of Oxford. The college I chose was called Wycliffe Hall. They were a great group of people and teachers. The Principal was Julian Thornton-Duesberry, which is a very interesting name. He was connected with the Moral Re-Armament Movement. He was a very kind, godly type of person. I was only 23-years-old when I went there, so I'm sure he wasn't much over 60 but he seemed to be well over 70! I lived in there. I enjoyed the time very much indeed.

Romances

Whilst I was at Reading, I had gone home to Egham every night and helped in the local church, and so got a chance to get to know a girl called Pat. At first I thought she was the one for me! However, after the first few months at Wycliffe College, when I talked about going to the Arctic, she truly got cold feet. That was the end of that relationship!

God had a much more dedicated person planned for me – Margaret Joan Porter. In the fall of 1954, someone whose name I've forgotten introduced us to each other. I had been beginning to wonder about my need to have a future partner who would not get "cold feet" about going to live with me in the Arctic – also someone who would share my sense of vocation. It was a joy to know that there was this someone – Margaret! We first met on Oxford Station after we'd corresponded a bit. Love at first sight! Our first date was from the station to a teashop. I remember that teashop, and we had tea, toast and jam and got talking. Afterwards, I took her to a very Evangelistic type of meeting. Then I took her back to the station. What a different courting pattern from today's dating practices! We continued to date nearly every week-end. She also went with me, when I had to go and take services in a small country church near Oxford, in a village called Towersey. This was good practice for me and also a good introduction for her to know what she would be in for!

We clicked! She was brave enough, after she realized where I was going, to say that she would go with me to the Arctic – how thankful I was when I heard her say this. We got engaged on December 31, 1954. Next, I had to go to meet her parents, who lived in a country village called Frith Common, which is between Birmingham and Worcestershire in the middle of England. That was quite an experience for me, because there they had no lights, no running water and used an outhouse. That was a test for me, as to whether I could adapt to different conditions of living. Growing up in the High Street in Egham we had every-thing, so it was quite different at Frith. I think her father was rather suspect of me, because he'd had poor past experiences with clergy. Margaret was the only child, and here's me talking about going to the Arctic with her, and taking her away from her parents in England. Her dad had lost Margaret's mom, because Margaret's mother died as a consequence of having being in-fected with polio when Margaret was only three years-old. Her dad remarried; I think it was a fairly good relationship between her dad and her stepmother. Margaret found it extremely hard to have a good relationship with her stepmother. She loved her dad very much so there was no problem there, and her dad loved her very much also. Good in one way, another way of course, for me to be the one taking her away from them – that was a no-no! Hard to say whether they were really church people, but like my father, they did not understand why I would want to go. Mar-garet's stepmother, who Margaret called "Aunt," was the person who loved the Chapel, which was very near their home, next door to a Pub!

We went several times to stay with them before the time would soon be when it was necessary for us to depart for Canada.

CHAPTER 2: THE FIRST POSTING— LAKE HARBOUR (KIMMIRUT)

Slated to Go to Kimmirut

I was ordained Deacon in Southwark Cathedral. That was in June of 1955, after I had scraped through my theological exams. I did very poorly in Doctrine at Wycliffe Hall. That's a bad thing to not be doing well at! I always thought that if we had only two years in theological college, we got the rest of our lives to study theology. God would understand, but not people! After the ordination, we went back to my home in Egham. Margaret stayed there and the next day she went to her home at Frith Common and said goodbye to her parents. It was a hard time for her dad, knowing that his only daughter, who he dearly loved, was going away and going away for a five-year period! She was very brave to go and face her dad and stepmother with this news!

In the words of the Bishop of the Arctic, Bishop Donald Marsh, I was "slated to go to Lake Harbour" (as it was called then – now called Kimmirut). Margaret was "slated" to go to Pangnirtung, also on Baffin Island, but over 300 miles away and with no road connection. The Bishop did not want us in the same place because we were not yet married!

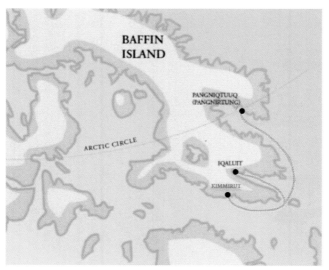

Kimmirut and Pangnirtung, on Baffin Island

We had to sign up for five years, to these places to which we had never been before, and agree to stay there. This was a real test for our faith. Also, before going to Canada, we had to make a requisition for the food we were going to eat the coming year when we were in the North. We used the Hudson Bay Company staff's requisition forms. There were suggested amounts on that form that we could order, but we were told they were rather too generous amounts for missionaries, so we had to cut down. If we didn't cut down, there'd be somebody who would do it for us – the Bishop! He personally looked at our requisition forms to see what we'd ordered, and acted accordingly. We could not order any fresh fruit, vegetables or fresh or frozen meat, but only canned and dried goods, as all perishables would spoil during transportation and not keep after delivery, even if they made it that far. This was all a real challenge – let alone to guess what you'd be eating in a "foreign place" for the next year after you finally arrive at your Mission!

As well, there was a long list of items we had to take with us – it all seemed such a lot of stuff. We had to buy yards and yards of material to use later as barter material for buying caribou skins for our parkas –these were the best type of parka when travelling, better than any cloth material. We also had to buy "Grenfell cloth" as a cover for a non-travelling parka. This non-travelling parka would be tailored using duffle that the Hudson's Bay Company (HBC) sold. When you're around the community, you don't want to dress up in furs, but when you're on the trail they are nice and warm and keep you cozy, as if you're the animal itself. So that's what we had to barter for. I remember Margaret and I went to a sort of an odd place in London, especially to buy trunks in which to start packing all our effects. The trunk store was in a dark passageway. I think when the guy found out where we were going, he almost gave us the trunks! That was an adventure, and a rush to get our stuff ready to go. I think it was about only eight or nine days in which to get ready, after I had left Wycliffe Hall, before leaving for Canada – just over a week between being ordained Deacon and when we had to say our final goodbyes.

Saying goodbye was not easy. My mother was living on her own in Egham while I was at College. I was the only one who had been living with her, and I had to say goodbye for five years. My mother had Parkinson's disease. When I left her, the departing wasn't as terrible as I thought it might have been, as she accepted the fact that I needed to fulfill my calling. However, I had a deep-down feeling of sorrow having to leave her, although I knew that this was part of the cost to my being called to the Arctic. We only found out later that she eventually had to be put into a nursing home, after having first moved back to Woolston with my father. I guess it worked out that she couldn't stay on her own because of the Parkinson's disease. They had separate bedrooms. I am sure that she must have had a hard time living at Woolston, although it might have got a bit better after her mother-in-law died around 1958.

I believe my father had begged Margaret not to go with me. He thought that if she wouldn't go, neither would I. I felt so sorry for my father. He even begged us not to go as we were wait-ing on Egham Station Platform to board our train bound for London (to catch a further train from there going to Liverpool Docks). He did it with the best intentions and even offering all the money he could think of, if we stayed in England. I had this deep conviction that we had to go whatever the cost. Even if we were not given money, never mind, as long as we could do what we felt was the Lord's will. It didn't seem right, humanly speak-ing, to go to a faraway place, never been to, very cold, leaving our parents – my father kept on saying, "You'll freeze to death." There was an inner war going on. We very much prayed about the whole situation and felt convinced to go ahead.

Ironically, we almost "froze to death" when we came back on holiday to England! We found the English homes so cold, espe-cially the older homes. We were quite warm in our homes in the Arctic. The Lord looks after you for sure!

In late June 1955, the Diocese of the Arctic had booked our pas-sage on the Cunard Line. The Bishop did not want us to go on the same boat together, let alone live in the same place, before we were married. So he had arranged to get Margaret on one boat and me on another boat. That's what his plan was! However, we twisted the arm of the Cunard Line agent, and he was very kind and agreed to put us both on the same boat. The boat we would have gone on was the *Franconia*, but because of various strikes we were to be diverted to the *Saxonia*. I think we boarded it in sort of a quiet way, because of this strike going on in Liver-pool. Our baggage of those two trunks and other items, we had sent on ahead of us to Liverpool Docks. Our train from London did take us right up to the Docks, and we just had to wait there to get to the *Saxonia*. We first had to board a special little tug-boat which took us out to the *Saxonia*, anchored away from the Docks because of the strike.

As we waited on the dockside, we could see people's baggage bound for the *Saxonia*, being loaded up onto various little boats. We were worried as to whether our baggage that we had sent on ahead had caught up with us. To this day, we can remember how very thankful we were to see one bit of baggage that we recognised was ours – that was my dark red piano accordion case with the accordion inside! I had packed the accordion because I can't sing for the life of me. The only way to help with a hymn would be to play with my one finger reading the music written in a hymn book. We saw the accordion case actually being taken off the dockside and put onto a cargo barge. We were very relieved! We then boarded the *Saxonia* from the smaller boat and settled in to our separate cabins. It was quite a rough passage! I always used to say, "The rougher the better," but Margaret didn't like the rough sea, and I don't think I saw her until we almost got to the St. Lawrence River. She was so seasick the whole way and stayed in her cabin more or less the whole time. I believe the Bishop did still have his way in the end!

We did meet someone on the boat who was going to be very helpful to us later, Dr. Ward. He was a professor at Wycliffe College in Toronto. So we got to get to know him and his family. He gave us many good tips and much inspiration. Well, we got to the St. Lawrence River and arrived in Québec City. There was a strike by the dockers who worked at loading and unloading the liners in Montreal. We would've docked in Montreal, but had to go to Québec City instead. We arrived on July the 1st, 1955, and there we got our train to Montreal, then another train from Montreal to Toronto, because Toronto was the headquarters of the Diocese of the Arctic.

We were again separated – Margaret and me! Margaret was sent to Georgina House (a home for single ladies, as it was designated) and I was going to be billeted at the Church Army there in Toronto. Captain Ray Taylor was in charge – a very fine Christian person who was going to look after me there. Besides the kindness I received, I still remember the breakfasts that were served, which gave me the first introduction to our custom here of drinking plenty of apple juice. In those days in the UK, it was never the custom to have apple juice with meals, except at certain fancy restaurants, when you would get a sample sized glass of it – good for only two gulps down!

Margaret and I were amazed how large the portions of food were in Canada, after having come from the small and bleak servings of the UK. When we were on the train to Toronto, I can remember we had a huge portion of Chicken à la King – it seemed a feast for the King! I guess that after the rationing in England, the meal on the train seemed such a big contrast. I remember it was only $2 for the Chicken à la King and the other things going with it.

The lady who met us in Toronto was Mildred Johnson, and another name we had for her was "The Rock of Gibraltar." We believed she kept the whole Diocese going. She was a very tall, kind person, yet very astute. She took us to Murray's Restaurant for our first meal in a Canadian restaurant. I don't remember what we had, but anyhow she was really kind to do that.

We stayed then in these two different places, in Georgina House and Church Army, trying to get our bearings to live in Canada, but we didn't at first . We found it so hot – I remember the thermometer reached 100 degrees Fahrenheit (we didn't use Celsius then). We were invited to Bishop Marsh's house and stayed the whole day there. I know that we just sat in the basement because it was so hot elsewhere. I guess the purpose of going there was for us to get to know him and his wife, Mrs. Marsh. I expect the Marshes said to each other: "Oh no! What have we got here? – they will never make it!" The Marshes had two daughters, Valerie and Rosemary, and one son, David. I do not remember him being there at that time.

I know that after we had arrived in Canada, the following Saturday, Bishop Marsh took us for a trip in his car to Niagara Falls. The intense heat was even worse there – it was suffocating to us! I don't think we enjoyed that trip very much. Coming back in the car he suddenly spilled the beans and said, "Mike, on Monday you're going to start going to Lake Harbour! You better get ready!" Margaret would have to stay on in Toronto until she could get on a boat to this place on Baffin Island called Pangnirtung. We would be separated again – this time for two years (as we thought then).

Miss Johnson, the Diocesan secretary and the Rock of Gibraltar, didn't like my writing – too illegible – it took her a morning to decipher one letter from me! I don't know what it'd be like now – probably even worse. She said that I had to have a typewriter and I would get it at Eaton's store, but the next day was Sunday. In those days there'd not be a store open on a Sunday. However, she would not take "No" for an answer. This Miss Johnson, with her clout, somehow persuaded Eaton's store to open, especially to sell me that one typewriter! To open Eaton's store on a Sunday was unheard of then. That's the typewriter that went to the Arctic and which I used, so that Miss Johnson could read and understand my letters.

On the Monday I had said goodbye to Margaret. No way would the Bishop allow us to be in the same community. She was slated to go to the St. Luke's Anglican Mission Hospital in Pangnirtung as cook. This was to replace the cook, Willy, who was going out from Pangnirtung for a year's holiday. It had to be a year, as there was no means of transportation available then, to get her back in a lesser time. Margaret had to wait in Toronto until the *C.D. Howe* sailed from Churchill to go North –this was a hospital boat that would visit all the communities in the Eastern Arctic. Margaret would have to first go by train to Churchill from Toronto to catch the boat.

I was going a different way, because I was going to St. Paul's Anglican Church in Lake Harbour (now called Kimmirut), and so

I was not going on the *C.D. Howe*. Instead, I was going to go on the Hudson Bay Company's resupply boat, the *Rupertsland*. To get there, I had to take a train to Roberval via Montreal. I don't think I knew what was going on. Never had been on an overnight train, but I knew I had to stay sleeping overnight until I arrived in Montreal and then Roberval. At Roberval, I had to get on a DC3 airplane –in those days there were no jets. That DC3 was going to take me to Kuujjuaq (or rather Fort Chimo, as it was called then). The DC3 was quite an old crate, I'm sure. It seemed to me they tied up the door with string! There was no toilet except a "honey bucket" at the back of the plane, not very private and all new to me. That was the first plane that I'd been on, other than the time I was in the Air Force, when I had been up for a joy-ride twice in a little Oxford plane. But the first commercial flight I'd ever flown on was that one from Roberval to Kuujjuaq.

Map of Kuujjuaq in northern Québec

Well, we made our way without incident to Kuujjuaq and landed there. We were told "There's a forest fire on." Wow! A forest fire in the Arctic? That didn't seem possible, but it turned out that everyone was asked to go and help put this forest fire out. That included me – a real rookie, just arrived! We were successful!!

The person who met us in Kuujjuaq was the Reverend Jamie Clarke, who later became Bishop Clarke. He came to meet us in his very heavy metal boat, which he moored to the river bank.

Anyway, he was ahead of the times, because people nowadays have metal boats – aluminum boats. The metal on his boat seemed to weigh a ton! I think I had my heart in my mouth as we crossed the Kuujjuaq River in his boat to get to his house on the other side of the river, the Anglican Mission House. The idea of staying with him, besides waiting for the Rupertsland, was to start to get acclimatized to the North. He was very kind and patient with this rookie! He had no wife in those days. There was also another minister waiting there whose name was David Ellis. He was slated to go to Salluit on the Northern Québec coast.

David was going to come along with Jamie, the Bishop and myself, after the Bishop had eventually arrived on the *Rupertsland*. I found it all intriguing whilst waiting. In those days there were Cree Indians there in Kuujjuaq as well as Inuit. It was my first experience meeting either race and to hear their singing. I thought how slowly they sung, but beautifully. It seemed that their singing voices showed a lot of devotion and worship in them. I went to all the services that were on. Jamie had to preach and know a bit of Cree as well as Inuktitut (Inuit language) so that he could accommodate both races.

He fed us while we were there. I can only remember dill pickles and beets! He seemed to have a lot of those stored in big glass jars, but I don't remember what else we had. I'm sure some of the food was different from what I'd been used to, but it was a good introduction to the North. There were no fresh fruit or vegetables! I had to try and pick up a few Inuktitut words and brush up more on my syllabics. Before I even arrived in Kuujjuaq I was trying to learn the syllabic characters used to write Inuktitut; I did that by use of flashcards. That system was something I learned of whilst I was in University. Inuktitut is a language that is very accommodating to syllabics, which is a short way of writing the language down. The problem was that of dialect – in Kuujjuaq the Inuit language that's spoken there has a different dialect from Baffin Island, to where I was going, It'd be a bit like northern England dialect compared with southern England dialect.

In those days whilst in Kuujjuaq, I was introduced to various people and even in those days my memory wasn't the best because I was introduced to the same guy three times -- I think it was Johnny May. That was embarrassing!

When the *Rupertsland* had finished unloading, it was time to depart to be on its way to Kimmirut. There was Bishop Marsh, Dave Ellis, Jamie Clarke and myself, all on that *Rupertsland* boat. It didn't go directly to Kimmirut. It first called in at another place called Payne Bay (now Kangirsuk), and there it anchored. People then were in tents. No such thing as a snow house in mid-July. I think I was very surprised. I thought it would be much colder, but it wasn't, and it seemed to be rather pleasant, except for the hordes of mosquitoes.

Then we arrived and anchored fairly early in the morning. I'm never a morning person and I was greeted by parishioners around 6:30 in the morning. I still had my PJs on! That was my first introduction to them and them to me. It was an amazing place. What was then Lake Harbour is now called Kimmirut, which means "That which makes a heel." It has this name because there's a formation of rock that looks like a great heel of a foot, right there in the main part of the harbour. You can see this in the picture of it:

Kimmirut's "Heel"

Kimmirut the morning I arrived (July 26 1955)

Kimmirut Mission House

So I got off the boat and was taken to the Mission House in a freighter canoe. The house was built in 1946, well-made out of the usual wooden building materials. I was agreeably surprised as to how nice it was. It had a small kitchen with a coal-fired kitchen range for cooking and heating the house. There was also a separate small living room and what, to my shame, was called a "Native Room" by the Bishop and Diocese. That room was meant for Inuit visitors when they came to our house, where they would sit around drinking tea and eating pilot biscuits. Then there were two bedrooms at the top of a steep flight of stairs. Upstairs, there were storage spaces all the way along both sides of the house under the eaves. It was in these spaces that we kept our canned food and Wind Charger batteries.

There was no running water, no flush toilets, and no electrical power available, as we did not have a generator. To get water, in the summer, I had to go with a bucket, walk 300 metres, and put the bucket under a pipe that had running water coming from a small waterfall above it. Then I would cart this water to the Mission House and pour it into a 10-gallon water container there. Hot water had to be heated up on top of the stove. I don't think I had a daily bath there! In winter I had to keep melting snow to fill up a 45-gallon drum for my washing water – that was a lot of snow! In winter you had to have a large melting container for the big volume of snow that you needed in order to get enough washing water. Later, after we were married, I ordered a very long hosepipe that went from the stream to our house. That gave us all the cold water we needed – but we could only use this system in summer before freeze-up. Even so, it seemed a luxury to us!

The house had a bit of furniture in it, and Bishop Marsh had insisted that we didn't have too much furniture. There was a sofa, an easy chair and a table with four chairs in our living room. The Diocese called a carpet a luxury – not for missionaries! – so it was all lino on the floors. For bedside tables we had orange crates turned up on their side. For the toilet, we had the infamous "honey bucket." This was a big pail – without a plastic bag, as none had been invented in those days. Every morning I would go down to the sea and discharge the contents – that was our sewage system.

You might wonder how I really felt when I first arrived in Kimmirut and saw how I would be living for my first Arctic winter. Somehow, I was not apprehensive at all. I was thankful that we had finally arrived to live in an Arctic Mission. I was happily surprised that there was already a Mission House built and ready for me to live in. I had felt the need to answer God's call to the Arctic ever since I was 12 – and here I was, starting to fulfill that call, BUT I had so much to learn ahead of me!

I saw the food I was inheriting – all at least three years old. It was stored under the eaves inside of the house. It was all canned stuff, which I had to buy, as that was a Diocesan rule. You bought food already there in cans at a discount – the amount of discount was based on how old the food was. This was food left over from the last missionary's supplies. The last guy was the Reverend Ruskell. Bishop Marsh called him "Ruskell the Rascal." This was because he was very High Church, went around the community in a cassock and had a biretta. He dressed up in formal dinner-wear clothes for his supper, even when he was eating alone. He called the Communion service "Mass." None of this went down very well with the locals – or the Bishop!

Part of this "food inheritance" was those Maple Leaf brand three-pound oblong cans of bacon. These were great long cans of mostly fat bacon, with little bits of lean bacon in. There was a can or two of chicken as well. We were supposed, however, to get and eat local food, although there wasn't really any caribou meat to eat locally. The caribou had gone away 20 years or so ago, on their big circuit of mid and South Baffin, and it was rare to get them near to the community. There was some seal meat, Arctic hare, ducks and ptarmigan that were available to eke out the canned foods. I had to start getting used to these "alternative menu" items. The bulk of the alternative menu seemed to be raw seal meat! I remember that a Lay Helper, Davidee, brought me a little bit of it in a cup – I wondered what I was going to do with it. I thought I would cook it up. When you do this, unless you know what you are doing, you get a strong seal scent. I did not like that too much, because I did not know how to cook it. When cooked properly it makes a very fine stew. If you eat it raw, it can be hard to chew, but you get used to its unique taste. When you are cold, there is nothing better than to chew a bit of raw seal meat, dripping with warm blood, to get yourself warmed up! In those days I did not know how seal meat has a complete range of vitamins to keep you healthy – including Vitamin C (the only meat that has this vitamin). I am thankful to this day for Davidee, who initiated me into this wonderful food.

After the three other clergy had left, the next morning I woke up to the sound of dishes being washed in the kitchen sink. I was scared and wondered who had come into the house. No one locked their doors in those days! Couldn't do that today, but then you never locked a door. There was a lady there called Annie. It turned out that she was doing the dishes. I didn't ask her to, she just did it of her own accord. She had come into the Mission House early in the morning. Her husband's name was Mingeriak. It turned out that the husband was also a Lay Helper in the Church. He was one also who tried to teach me Inuktitut. He must have been very patient!

All our supplies had come off the boat and were in good order. I put them away in various places, including the coal that I had to purchase out of my $2000 per year salary. That was purchasing the coal for the kitchen and Native Room stoves, which burnt coal – and I also sometimes used it for the Church stove.

For our electrical power we used wind power. We were really with it! Wind power in those days! I remember that it wasn't working when we got there with Bishop Marsh. I had to wait before some replacement generator could be shipped in to repair the Wind Charger. This would only arrive in the Christmas mail drop in December. It was only a 12-volt system and charged six 2-volt batteries. When there was a big wind, you really could hear the batteries bubbling away, almost as though the Wind Charger was going to take off and the whole house go up in the air. But it worked whilst there was wind. In those days there didn't seem to be so much wind as there is today. When there was no wind, there'd be no power and no lights! We were so dependent upon that wind, but it was good while it worked. On calm winter days we used kerosene lamps, which were lit by lighting a type of wick mantle, which soaked up kerosene from a glass bowl. In addition, there was a pressure lamp that used gas and had a mantle to light up in the middle. Never had lit one in my life before this!

A gas-powered pressure lantern (Qimmirkbee's) – like
the one that nearly blew up on me!

One day when we had no juice left in the batteries from the Wind Charger, I saw this gasoline lamp and there was no mantle or anything on it, so I thought a flame would come out of the pipe and I, in my real stupidity, tried to light the flow of air coming out of that pipe from this gas lantern. But by a miracle, and I'm sure it was a miracle, I couldn't light it! Yet there was my lighted match, which could easily have made the whole thing explode in my face, but it never did. Thank the Lord for that!

St. Paul's Anglican Church, Kimmirut, and its Parishioners

When it came time for Church on a Sunday, there was a bell tolled from the Church spire – I guess it came from an old CPR train. As soon as the bell was rung, then you would see the people coming to Church from all directions with their little bags of hymn and prayer books and Bibles. These books that the Inuit used were already translated into Inuktitut syllabics by previous missionaries. Later on, however, I learnt that not all of these translations were fully understood, as they were very much in another dialect. Anyhow, there was enthusiasm. There was no one who played the organ. Services were all held without an organ playing and people sang very slowly. A little laboured, shall we say? The trouble is that I'm not a singer either! I hope the Lord accepted our singing as it was then.

It seemed that there were only three people in charge of running the services in the Church. There was Mingeriak, who I mentioned earlier, Davidee and Anogak. There was no choir or anything like that. One of the three would start off the singing – or rather, one of the wives did! Almost the whole community would be in the Church Sunday by Sunday. I read out parts of the service as best as I could with my English accent. It was not long before I had to lead nearly all of the service. It must have been a bit painful for the people listening to my halting Inuktitut! The people there were very patient and kind to be welcoming me and let me be part of their spiritual lives. They knew that I was very anxious to learn the language and culture.

Anogak, a Lay Helper (there is a picture of Davidee elsewhere, with wedding group pictures – unfortunately I do not have a picture of Davidee's brother, Mingeriak)

An interesting Parishioner: Iperkvik

Bishop Marsh had told me that he did not expect me to do anything other than to learn the language and be with the people – to get to know their customs and ways. That was wise advice! I wasn't burdened down with meetings and things like that.

That is not the end of the story, though. Bishop Marsh also told me that he expected me to preach my first sermon in Inuktitut on the first Sunday that I was in Kimmirut – what a challenge! How did I do that?! I studied the English New Testament and tried to put various verses together and connect them to make a very short talk. Then I looked up the equivalent verses in the Inuktitut New Testament, which were written in syllabics. Then I wrote these verses out in roman orthography. Then I read out the roman script on the first Sunday I was there, not having a clue as to what I was saying! I shudder to think what it must have sounded like. I think people were very kind to accept me and my halting sermon. I am sure the congregation did not understand what I said. But at least it showed them that I was in earnest to be there and get to know them and their language and culture. I did soon get used to reading syllabics, in a month or so, because they are fairly simple to learn and help avoid writing out great long words in the roman script.

---

vi   SYLLABARIUM

over the characters in the third column lengthens the vowel sound to *oo*, as *oo* in the word *good*; e.g. *oo* ᐳ, *poo* ᐳ, *too* ᑐ, etc. Dotted characters in the fourth division are sounded as *a* in the word *far*; e.g. *a* ᐊ, *pa* ᐸ, *ra* ᕋ, etc.

2. DOUBLE CONSONANTS.

The nasal sound (almost expressed by our letters *ng*) is formed by the character ᖕ, while the guttural sound *rk* (almost *ark*) is expressed by the two small final characters ᖅ ᒃ.

EXERCISES.

Single Characters.

ᖃ, ᐃ, ?, ᐅ, ᐊ, ᒐ, ᐸ, <, ᐱ, >, ᐳ, ᐸ, <, ᖅ, ᓯ, ᕐ, ᐃ, ᐱ, ᐊ, ᓕ, ᐅ, ᐊ, ᓐ, ᐱ, ᐳ, ᐁ, ᐧ, ᐱ, ᕋ, ᔨ, ᒃ, ᒡ, ᑦ, ᑉ, ᕝ, ᕐ, ᐡ, ᐃ, ᑊ, ᐸ, ᐃ, ᓂ, ᕐ, ᐸ, ᐧ, ᐧᓖ, ᐧᐁ, ᓂ, ᔨ, ᕆ, ᒐ, ᓕ, ᐧ, ᐧᐧ, ᐃ, ᐃ, ᑊ, ᐃ, ᐸ, ᐧ, ᐧᓖ, ᐃ, ᖅ

(syllabic exercise characters)

SYLLABARIUM   vii

Short Words.

(syllabic text)

Short Words with Double Consonants and Finals.

(syllabic text)

Short Sentences.

(syllabic text)

The Lord's Prayer.

(syllabic text)

Instructional material for learning syllabics in the *Book of Common Prayer … Translated into the Eastern Arctic Eskimo Tongue*, originally published in 1960.

St. Paul's was a nice Church, built in 1946. It was not ornate. It was just like a usual Church with the Holy Table and the cross on the Table and two candlesticks, with wooden benches to seat the congregation. The Church was heated by a space heater fueled by some of the coal we had. It was bitterly cold when I had to light the heater in winter – it would freeze your butt off!

St. Paul's Anglican Church in Kimmirut, built in 1946

The Church had a sort of leadership. I found it very hard to work out who really was in charge. It didn't seem to be any pre-designated person, as far as the Lay Helpers went. These Lay Helpers weren't officially called "Lay Readers" (as they would have been called today, after they had been sufficiently trained beforehand). They were just Helpers. The Helpers, I thought, with the limited amount of Inuktitut that I understood, didn't seem to know very much - most of the sermon they said was telling people that they, the Lay Helpers, didn't know much! That wouldn't happen today, but the great thing about the Church was that the whole community came out on a Sunday whenever it was Church time. By "people" I mean children as well. I'm afraid I'm embarrassed to say there was no Sunday School. I don't remember even a choir. They just came as families and I somehow got to communicate to the Lay Helpers that they would lead and I wouldn't be able to do too much – although I did take parts of the service, just by reading the syllabics in the Prayer Book and New Testament. I gradually got into the whole spirit of the thing. I don't think there was much of a sermon by any of the Helpers or myself, but people came and they seemed happy there. It was very much a social thing to go to Church, even if you didn't get the real meaning. There were, however, quite a few committed Christians there.

People of Kimmirut

When I arrived in 1955 there were around 300 people. This included those in some near and far isolated fishing and hunting camps. However, when fox fur and sealskin pelt prices dropped way down, people started looking for other ways to make a living. Some were good carvers and sold their carvings to the Hudson's Bay Company (HBC), but not all could do this. Some took on work as boat builders in the summer. This was a project instigated by the HBC, and it employed about eight carpenters to build the boats. You can see a picture of this project:

HBC boat builders of Kimmirut!

When fall came, boat builders and some other Inuit there for the summer would return to their camps. This would leave only about 35 people in Kimmirut for the winter. There was the un-married HBC Manager, Gordon Rennie, who had his house near his small store (he had a non-Inuk clerk who also lived with him). Then there was his Inuk helper, Georgie, and family in a small staff house .There was also a tiny Nursing Station, with Bess Parsons as the Nurse. She and her husband Bill lived there together with their two sons Billy and David; later on she had a baby girl, called Gail. Bill and Bess had an Inuk helper to do the chores, who lived in a very small house. The Royal Canadian Mounted Police had a Detachment on the other side of the fiord where another member lived, Cliff Barr, together with his wife Michelle. They also had a helper, Special Constable Akavak and his wife and family. They were also responsible for a man named Silasee. He was mentally handicapped and had murdered his wife in Inukjuak. Silasee was free to roam around and do chores for the Police. That was all who were there in the winter – except when Christmas was coming!

My First Christmas in the Arctic

Christmas came around – a great time to meet up with families from far-away camps. They came into trade at the one HBC store as well as to celebrate Christmas. There was no community hall in Kimmirut, except an old rundown dance hall, which was a relic from when the Americans were there in the '40s during the war. The USAF had had a little out-station there as a branch of the DEW Line. As the Church was the only place to meet at Christmas time, people would come to the Church for the 11 o'clock service. When the service was over, there would be a big batch of what we would call "bean stew," brought to the Church. This stew was really a great conglomeration of everything people had donated to help make a stew. The Police would go around and get their donation of food items from the people living in Kimmirut. These had to fill about a 10-gallon vat. The RCMP and the HBC worked together, as the HBC manager there, Gordon Rennie, his clerk, and the two Police members would make the stew. Gordon was quite a character from Newfoundland and had worked with the HBC since he was 17. They all arranged to have the stew brought to the Church around 12:15, together with camp stoves, to brew up tea.

Whole families came dressed up in their parkas, bringing their enamel, rather chipped, mugs and maybe a spoon and a plate. There were no paper plates in those days. This great big vat of bean stew would then be doled out to the people. You'd think they'd never get through that 10 gallons of bean stew. There would be 200 or more people to feed sitting on benches in the Church, all crammed up together. It was quite a tight fit but it worked and people were very happy, laughing and joking away. A special time to celebrate! Nearly all had come in from their isolated camps and camped out in Kimmirut for this real festive occasion. The cold did not seem to bother them, as they had to sleep in tents in December. After I had been in Kimmirut for a year there was also a Nativity Play that I had organised. This is remembered to this day!

Our Nativity Play in St. Paul's Church, Kimmirut

Then, after that, people went to the various places where they were staying – later on they would all troop down to the sea ice. There we played outdoor games, maybe races or some sort of wrestling games or various contests of skill and strength, where everyone laughed and had fun and enjoyed it. Then another service in the evening. After we had been there for a second Christmas, we had more organized activities and games. After Christmas people would go back to their various isolated camps. They had come in before Christmas with their dog teams – the dogs in the community of Kimmirut were all howling to greet the dogs coming in from the camps. Over Christmas there were hundreds of dogs all tethered up and howling together, which made quite a grand symphony as they saluted each other. It seemed that there was always a clear moonlight night around that time of year. It was a very beautiful picture, with the light from the moon and stars reflecting off the pure white snow. There were in addition the sensational flickering coloured Northern Lights.

It was cold but we didn't mind that then! Altogether everything made it a very special Northern picture for Christmas.

I made some great friends there in Kimmirut and people who I'll never forget, most of whom I'm afraid are not living as I write this book.

Contacting Margaret

What was I going to do about Margaret? By this time, Margaret had been sent to Pangnirtung, after having waited in Churchill for the hospital and supply boat, the *C.D. Howe*. It was a six-week journey from Churchill to Pangnirtung, where she was going to be the cook. She was put there so we wouldn't have a "sinful relationship" in Kimmirut! Another reason was the Bishop's past experiences with those missionaries who had gone as married couples from the South: when the wife didn't like the North, they both had to quit. That had meant that the husband would go as well and return to the South. The Bishop lost his man because he had to follow his wife who didn't want to be in the North. So the Bishop had the idea that it would be best to let missionaries go North unmarried, and live in two different communities, apart from each other. Then if the woman did not like the North, the man would not be forced to go back South with her. At least that was his theory!

I wondered, "How am I going to contact Margaret if she's in Pangnirtung and I'm in Kimmirut, 300 miles apart?" The only way was by single sideband radio at the Hudson Bay Company. No such thing as a phone then and no scheduled flights either. Also there was no mail contact, other than by a Christmas mail drop and on the supply boat in summer. That was also a great joy to me when Christmas was about to come. You would see the plane come over the community and drop the mail by parachute.

I have to side-track to tell one story about this mail drop. The policeman's wife there in Kimmirut had ordered a dinner service set from Eaton's. When the parachute drop came, everything went fine, except for one parachute that failed to open – and as you might have guessed, her precious dinner set was in the basket attached to that parachute! Everything was shattered.

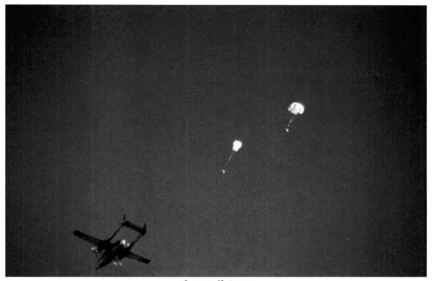

The Mail Drop

The whole Community got very excited when the mail-drop was coming. Catalogue orders and all the personal mail was coming – we would be in touch with friends and family again! The plane also dropped three or four Christmas trees, which landed upright in the snow and made them look as if they had been growing there all the time. It was great to get letters and for me to know that all was well with Margaret. You can imagine how lonely and concerned I felt at times. How was I going to contact her, keep in touch with her and things like that? Likewise my letters to her, which became almost a book, would she get them in her Christmas mail drop? She did!!

A Visit to a Camp and Local Food

After Christmas it was necessary to go and find out more about how Inuit lived, so I went just after Christmas to the camp that Mingeriak lived in. I had my fur parka by now, sewn by a lady called Aperkshoo, using the caribou skins that the Diocese had sent on the *Rupertsland*. I also had to have some Inuit winter sealskin boots, called ᐅᑉ (kamiik, often referred to by English speakers as kamiks), fur caribou skin mitts, and lots of other clothes. Then I had to take food: flour, baking powder, lard, sugar, tea, soap and some hard candies for the kids (don't tell the dentist!). I had no idea what I had to do, but Mingeriak was a help in getting my clothing together, as well as advising me about my rifle and the ammunition to take. So we set off over the barrier ice and onto the sea ice for about a four-hour journey. At one or two places on the trail, it meant we had to quickly get over some loose floating ice in order to carry on further. That made my heart go up to my rookie head! Looking down beside the floating ice pans you could see the black, icy seawater around the pan you had just jumped onto, as it moved up and down. Then jump onto the solid ice and the trail to follow – what a relief!

However, we arrived safely at Mingeriak's camp. We went into his winter tent or qammaq, as it was called. It looked quite civilised – it was a wooden structure with snow banked around it. There was also a 6-volt Wind Charger there. He was truly ahead of his time! There were his wife Annie, his daughters Koopa, Ningeoapik and Ida, as well as his son Padlo, all living there. It seemed a large building then, but many years later, when I went back to look at it the remaining skeleton of the house, it looked so small!

I picture Mingeriak waking me up at 5:30 in the morning and me getting dressed, having porridge, getting the dogs hitched up, rushing down over the barrier ice over a roughly worn trail, and going to the floe edge to go hunting. My job was just to stand over a seal hole and wait for the seal to come up and breathe and then shoot it. You mustn't make any movement whatsoever.

You've got to just wait until there's a stirring and a breathing. That's the seal coming up to get air! Don't move! Shoot! There the seal is, shot through the head. Hook him and pull him up through the breathing hole!

I wasn't very successful at hunting seals. I'm thankful Mingeriak was good at it, because it was a great occasion. When it got dark, we'd go back with the dog team to his camp, greeted by children and Elders there, unhitch the dogs from the ᖃᒧᑏᒃ (qamutiik: sled), cut up some old stored seal meat and throw it to the hungry, just-chained-up dogs; then into their qammaq, sit down and have seal meat – usually eaten almost immediately after arriving, so it was not cooked. People would be gathered in the qammaq and the whole seal would be cut open and gutted while all are there. The men who were cutting the seal open would scoop up a bit of still warmish blood to gulp down with their hands. This was the real way to get warm! Then, from the gutted seal lying on a piece of cardboard on the floor, some men would take off various pieces of rib, or gut, or brain, or eyes, to be shared with the women. Then all the men there would eat and finish off the rest of the animal, until only the blubber was left on the flattened out skin. Everyone was always very happy. When available, tea and bannock would follow.

Enjoying the healthiest food in the world – seal meat! (Martha and Oloota)

I had to learn to eat the food that Inuit liked and, of course this included a lot of raw seal meat, but I didn't get on to that very quickly!! So when staying in a camp I would be one of those squatting around the seal carcass getting to enjoy the company and the food. The meat kept me warm and nourished me fully – the fresh bannock was always an added treat!

I think that it is a very important point to note about their Inuit culture then, that you didn't save things for a rainy day. In their thinking, if you do, you become a mean person, a miserly person. You've got to share all of what you've got right away. I make a deliberate point about this, because I think that's a key to how people would act later on, when they were all together in a community and there was alcohol available. Often the aim today is still not to save any of the booze for later. You have got to drink it all up. If you put it aside for another day, you're a mean person. I believe having to "kill the bottle" makes for a lot of the drunkenness and things that we see these days. It's a sort of cultural thing, to finish the bottle like you would finish the seal. Of course there are many non-Inuit who also want to kill the bottle and get drunk with their friends, but for many other different reasons.

My First Hunting Experiences

Whilst I was at Mingeriak's place I wasn't always with him hunting. One day he left me on my own at the floe edge. The floe edge there was where the old sea ice ends and the new ice is forming, just attaching itself to the old stable thick ice. The new ice edge would be at least a foot below the old ice. The new ice formed overnight.

At the floe edge looking for seals

Gotileak sees a seal and shoots

Gotileak has to retrieve the seal that he just shot, paddling
this small boat to fetch it

There it is! Ready to take home for a feast!

I was getting bored whilst I was waiting there by my little lone-some self for any seal to suddenly pop up. A little sea pigeon sud-denly landed in the water very close to where I was standing. "Well, I'll have a pot shot at that! Something to do!" I hit it and it drifted towards me, in the still-open, little patch of water, near the new ice that had formed overnight. It drifted right up to this bit of new ice, so I thought, "Aha! I can go and get that!" I put my foot down from the old ice onto the new ice and it seemed okay. Another foot -- the bird was almost there for me to pick up – but my foot went right through that new ice! The other foot stayed on top of the new ice, so I didn't sink right into the sea. My guardian angel must have been there supporting me! I could then clamber back on to the old main ice – safe! But there was I, with nothing other than the caribou skin clothing which I had on, and which had got soaked up to my waist. What was I going to do? I think I just waited and prayed that something would happen.

Lo and behold, about three or four minutes after this, Qipaniq, who lived in the next door qammaq to Mingeriak, happened to be coming by with his dog team. He knew at once what had happened, jumped off his qamutiik, and got me wrapped around in caribou bedding that he had. Inuit always carry some caribou skins on top of their qamutiit, as well as sealskins. So I was able to go back quickly to his qammaq, where I got to thaw out my outer rock-hard frozen parka and pants -- but my legs were not frozen. That was a near escape!

Another time I was left to walk and hunt for ptarmigan, going up and down over hill and valley looking for them. I almost lost my way because there was little visibility, because of mist coming off the water. It was getting dark and here was I, not knowing where I was. But suddenly, as the mist seemed to clear, I could see lights in the distance. I knew they came from the people in Mingeriak's camp, but I had to get there. I had to get down onto the sea ice from the high, cliff-like piece of land, on which I was standing. I remember sliding down, not really seeing where I was going, onto the shore ice. This is the rough ice in between the main ice and the land. Luckily, the ice had solidified enough to support me. This shore ice is not always very safe either, when newly formed, just after high tides flow over the barrier ice onto it. However I made it back to the camp. What a relief!

Mingeriak and His Camp

There were two other families in their qammaqs. The one family was my rescuer Qipaniq's , and the other one was Matteoosie's. The latter was an old man – originally an RCMP Special Constable, retired long ago – who disliked qallunaat (white people -- I was one of them!). He was very protective of keeping Inuit culture to only Inuit people, so he didn't like me eating freshly caught uncooked seal meat, like an Inuk. I wouldn't therefore go to his qammaq to eat because of his views, although I did often go to Qipaniq's. I had to be very careful about not "treading on people's toes." I also of course held little services there in Mingeriak's qammaq with the three families (without Matteoosie!), as I gradually improved my Inuktitut. My whole experience with language and culture learning was like being thrown into the deep end. But I know now, although I didn't realise then, how the Lord was truly guiding and protecting me the whole time. Many of us come to realise this as we look back on our past lives!

I was at the camp for about six weeks. The sea ice wasn't very solid, because that was an extra-warm winter, even then. It meant that the ice got melted too much in certain areas, especially at high and low tide times during certain months. The tides would push the sea water up through various cracks and crevices in the barrier ice The overflow would make the ice around it very unstable and even break up all together. This happened while I was there at Mingeriak's camp; he couldn't go to trade in Kimmirut because the trail had got too broken up. Even with his good dog team, he couldn't do the trip to trade his seal skins and fox furs for necessary food and ammunition. At this time the camp ran out of, more or less, all of their supplies. The only thing they had left was flour and seal oil, so that meant eating some bannock that was made only with these two ingredients. Bannock was a type of scone cooked slowly over a qulliq (a seal oil lamp—also sometimes spelled "kudlik") with baking powder, salt, flour and lard or seal oil. That took a bit of getting used to, when it was made with seal oil. Even more so, it was hard when the baking powder and lard had run out – you were left with a stodgy portion of flour and seal oil!

Making bannock. Seal oil is added to flour and baking powder

It is then placed in a container and put over the qulliq to slowly cook

There we are – enjoying the freshly cooked bannock.

We had to wait until it was cold enough to be able to go to Kim-mirut. One day Mingeriak suddenly decided it was safe enough to go on the trail to Kimmirut to trade for supplies. He didn't want to take a scared rookie with him! I stayed there at his camp and spent the time, whilst he was away, shooting arctic hare and ptarmigan, to help out the food supply. What an excitement when Mingeriak came back with supplies – how extra precious were a pack of lard, some baking powder, a few hard candies, bullets for hunting, etc. We couldn't wait for the new baking powder bannock to be ready to eat – when cooked, it tasted wonderful!

After six weeks or so I went back to Kimmirut to check up on things and get refreshed and ready for more camp visiting. I'd go and visit two more local camps, but just staying two nights at each one.

Extracts From My Diary: Camp Stay With Mingeriak

Before proceeding any further, I thought that I should give you some extracts from my diary. I can thus better give you my actual thoughts at that time whilst I was at Mingeriak's camp. It will repeat a little of what I have already written, but it will help you to better feel my emotions of being a lone rookie qallunaat in an isolated camp and in a different culture. I have added a few extra comments not in my diary.

Extract from my diary, Thursday, December 29th of the year 1955: "Made my first journey by dog team to go to Mingeriak's camp, which is on a little strip of land in between two larger portions of land. On the way to his camp we stopped at another camp and we take a sack of coal with us for the one who was the leader of the camp. The man was called Napachi. He was one who takes services as well, so he became a good friend."

And then on Friday the 30th: "My first experience to go after seals: standing up with your feet apart over a seal hole. I hadn't put enough clothes on so I had to return back to Mingeriak's place, or qammaq as it is called in Inuktitut. I don't know what to call it really in English, a sort of cabin, but it's not really like a cabin that we think of. It was insulated with some bracken like plant in between the walls and the floor for insulation, covered over top and then snow blocks put around it. It was heated by kudliks -- a stone lamp or metal lamp. There were two or three of them so the place was warm as long as there was seal oil to burn in those kudliks. I had to return to get warmer clothes on."

The following is just a note I added in my diary. "I don't know why I didn't put enough clothes on, or why they didn't tell me I hadn't got enough, but did return to the seal hole after putting more clothes on, but there was no seal!"

"I wander around to keep warm but I'm always feeling a bit scared whether I am going to fall into the water. Because we would go where it was fairly newly formed ice and it would bend a bit under you. It wouldn't give way because it was very rubbery, not like fresh water ice. So I was fairly safe but I didn't feel that safe."

Then I see my next entry is January the 1st, 1956. I say, "Our YEAR!!" With that thought I wake up at 8 o'clock in the morning. Margaret and I will get married later on in this year!"

"Mingeriak and Annie always get up first. There's a stove in the qammaq and it seems to give out heat all night. There's also a Wind Charger for light." That meant a generator driven by the wind for power. It was only a 6 volt one, but at least it worked. "There were about two or three kudliks also that give out light and heat, burning seal blubber. Yesterday our neighbour Matteoosie had caught one seal and he gave us three-quarters of it and he kept the quarter. Then the rule seemed to be after that whoever gets one, he has it all. We rejoiced and even I rejoiced at the thought of some nice fresh seal meat. I would not like to live only on bannock. Would you?"

Monday the 2nd of January, 1956. "Wake up to a lovely day because the weather is good. It is decided we shall go seal hunting again. It seems that we wait for the decision of one man before we actually go. The eldest then decides to go and a sudden rush is made to get the dog team ready, to get the harness out, to unhitch the dogs, to place them so they can attach to the qamutiik or sled. Also when children visit a qammaq they seem to be chattering away in the entrance way. They don't usually come right inside to the bench where everyone is sitting down. The adults are sitting down on a very low wooden bench which is covered with skins and the children then in the porch entrance seem to be chattering away to each other, when all of a sudden they make a sudden dash to go outside. I don't know why but that's the way it always seemed to be."

"Mingeriak got two seals today and we have the meat for supper, cooked this time to make a stew. Just like beef, really nice. Later on in the evening dog harnesses are made and the sled, qamutiik, is mudded. I mean by that, that there's a coating of mud put on to the steel runner or wood runner of a qamutiik, is left to harden and freeze solid. When travelling it often gets damaged by rough ice. So it seems that quite often Inuit have to repair the damage done to the sled. Just before we could leave on the next day for seal hunting, it would mean having to put water, spat out onto the runners with a piece of bear skin, so that you would get a slippery surface over the mudded runners. If you just had mud without the ice on top of the mud, the mud would not make the qamutiik go very well - the dogs would not like that, neither would we!"

"This was all new to me and I had to try and learn their way of living and at times it was very hard to understand what really was going on because, remember, I've only been here six months or so and had to learn the language with no real help or book or anything like that. The Bishop had insisted that I never would use an interpreter in Church or out of Church. I had to learn the hard way, but it turned out to be the best way! I did have Reverend Peck's dictionary but you can't suddenly look up a dictionary in the middle of a conversation!"

"On Tuesday the 3rd of January got up at the very unearthly hour of 5 a.m. Wind seems to be not bad so it should be all right but it changes at 6 o'clock. If there's too much wind you can't hear the breathing of the seal when he or she comes up to breathe at their breathing holes. After finally getting away, pulled by Mingeriak's dog team over the barrier ice, then on to old ice, and finally onto the new ice where the seal holes are. I find three good holes but no luck. Not one is caught by any of our camp people but they're still optimistic. We return with nothing and take the time once we're back to fetch water, visit other qammaqs, eating bannock and seal meat from yesterday. But it doesn't seem to me to be monotonous. It seems that I'm trying to learn so it keeps me very interested."

One of the last qayaks used for hunting by Inuit

And the next day, Wednesday the 4th: "Again try for seal. Mingeriak gets one. Eaten by all raw. I didn't mind that but I didn't eat as much as they ate. The whole camp comes in to Mingeriak's qammaq and the bits of seal meat are passed around and the meat cut off with an ulu." An ulu is an Inuit type of woman's half-moon-shaped knife.

Thursday the 5th: "Sudden decision by Mingeriak to go after foxes by laying down traps for them spread out over a large area around his camp." Trading fox furs was big business, especially in the '30s when they were more greatly valued than later on. Fox trapping was a method of getting supplies to trade with for flour, baking powder, ammunition, household items and even for boats. "As I only have one pair of winter boots, I don't go." I don't know why I only had one pair. I wasn't prepared in some ways. Also I had got no instructions as to how I should be prepared. "Instead I'd try on my own to go after getting ptarmigan and rabbits. I see one ptarmigan but no luck. I nearly get lost and sleep outside during the night. I am really confused and praying to be guided to know the way to go. There! I saw in the distance some tiny light -- I realized it was the camp light! But how to get there? I had stupidly come a long way away. Well, it looked that I would have to get way down onto the sea ice and cross over to the camp. I had to do something which was very rash. I started sliding down on my behind down onto the Qaingoo." This is the seawater that comes up at a very high tide between the barrier ice and the land and then (hopefully!) gets frozen over and walkable (ᖃᐃᖑᒃ: qainguk). "Well, after a scary slide downhill onto the Qaingoo, I was relieved that it supported me and was frozen sufficiently. Walked over the barrier ice onto the main ice and crossed safely over to the camp. I was sure glad to get back there! Everyone else treated my adventure as just a little bit of experience of no consequence!"

"In the evening people all come in and play various games and contests, mainly strength ones, and sometimes go outside to play a game of pretend polar bears or ghosts, to hide, jump out and scare you. I got to know a bit about the game but not fully. And Friday, a lovely day. Looking for ptarmigan and rabbits. Tried shooting a ptarmigan four times but it got away. You see why I'm thankful the Lord didn't make me a hunter! I need different glasses!"

"Got back there to the camp to find Ningeorapik, she is Mingeriak and Annie's eldest daughter, and she'd caught a rabbit. How nice it was, although cooked with its head on. Qipaniq, that's one of the next door neighbours, returns with a fox. That would be his to be able to trade at the Hudson Bay Company. And Mingeriak returned with nothing. I'd go and visit Qipaniq next door and look at photos he's got."

Wednesday the 11th: "Mingeriak tries to build a new qamutiik. Works at it all day amidst snow, rain and strong winds, but the winds are very warm ones. We're happy of course to have wind, because the wind charger really buzzes around and by doing that charges up batteries and makes our lights brighter in the qammaq. In the evening, there's much merriment around Qipaniq's gramophone. Everyone seems very happy. Plenty of seals are now here. Dogs are fed and fat. No thought that snow might cause difficulty to hunt later."

On Wednesday the 12th: "Mingeriak departs at 6 a.m. to his older brother's camp. That would be 60 miles away and Mingeriak hadn't finished his work on the qamutiik, but he then had to borrow one, which must have been embarrassing for him to go there to his older brother's, Davidee . There's always a feeling of depression after the man of the house leaves and all is quiet, but in a way how much more restful for me. More time to think and to pray. Mingeriak only took bannock, jam and water for tea. Nothing else. That amazes me, and we ourselves ran out of baking powder which is a necessity to do a proper bannock." I don't seem to have provided anything. I'm wondering what I took to help out with the food. I shudder to think some of the things I did or did not do as a rookie. It's amazing how kind they were to accept me as I was!

On the 15th: The excitement when visitors come, especially from Lake Harbour, seems much keener to hear even the smallest amount of news and to receive the little letters put in syllabics. It's when you got everything, you don't especially notice them, but when you don't have them, the things that you did take for granted; when you don't have them, you really appreciate them when you do have them. And I noticed that Mary and Eeyeetseak have brought their own good supply of coffee and powdered milk and other goodies. What a treat! How much more you appreciate things after you go without. I sure did. There's a constant hustle and bustle back and forth as if everyone does a sudden exit on one accord, in and out of the door, just to go outside. Have lots of little games, dressing up and the kids playing with their inunguaq (their dolls made out of wood and little clothes to dress them up in), playing mothers and fathers, playing and imitating dogs." There were other games which I didn't write down or didn't understand.

Monday 16th: "I got to the floe edge, spot a seal within inches away. As usual I'm too late to get at it, to get my rifle and set it up to shoot. I kill a sea pigeon later and I do this at the floe edge. Kill it in water. It drifts in the current to the edge of the newly formed ice just below the edge of the old ice. Me on the main ice, I step down onto this newly formed ice just to test it. All seems well. Another step, okay and then another step my foot goes through the newly formed ice. That gave me a real scare! Helpless feeling. Managed to go backwards somehow. I'm sure the Lord or His angel helped me and I was able to grab on to the main ice ledge, pull myself up on to the main ice, pushing myself to near exhaustion. But soon our neighbour, Qipaniq came by with his dog team. I was tied onto the qamutiik with my wet pants and boots and Qipaniq wrapped me up in caribou fur and off we went back to our camp. Even the dogs knew, it seemed, that they must hurry. I had real joy when I reached the humble qammaq, got warm and thawed, fed tea and bannock."

"Then Mingeriak returns. 'Has he got foxes? Hope he has some baking powder!' These were our thoughts. I don't know whether more pleased to see him or the hoping for what he had brought!"

On the 18th: "We go visiting to another camp, Napachie's, and have a good qamutiik ride over bad ice." On the 19th: "The sun shines for the first time through the qammaq's window – there's great excitement. Mingeriak goes to Lake Harbour to trade foxes, so he must have got some. I don't know how many, but it meant he could buy flour and baking powder and bullets. That would be at the Hudson Bay Store in Lake Harbour."

Then "we have an outdoor game at night. One person pretends to be the bear and I didn't really see the purpose of what it was all about – something to do with marriage purposes." Now I do not guess!

On the 20th: "Think of Margaret and wish she was here. I went seal hunting. Mingeriak got one. Me, none again. Started feeling annoyed and embarrassed that I could not catch one. The Inuit really walk as they try to look for holes in the newly formed sea ice. They walk a long way. I feel really exhausted. Would like some time for peace and quiet, reading and letter writing. I'm beginning to miss food and keep thinking of it."

On the 21st: "I notice that Inuit also have bad tempers at times over nothing – to me apparently nothing. We set off really early. Annie gets two seals. One of those two seals has a fetus of a baby seal in it. The fetus was used as a plaything for Pudlo. That's their youngest. Plays with it. There's no disgust because it's a dead seal. I thought that what else would you use? This type of toy is called OO-KHOO-KHAA [ᐅᑯᖄ: uukuuqaa] and seems to give hours of entertainment. It's amazing, I thought, how the Inuit have adapted to the circumstances they are in and really are independent, except for this need to have bannock and, obviously a boat, baking powder, flour and things like that."

On the 24th: "I get my first ptarmigan, two of them. How happy am I!! Finally got something. Hardly had to walk to get one as I killed it at point blank range. The other was far off. There's an air of depression when no seal is caught and I also was depressed with myself that I couldn't catch one. Things you say are taken the wrong way but it soon lifts."

The 25th: "I got climbing up to the top of a high hill. I feel I have gone up to heaven. It's so like the setting that must've been for the Transfiguration. There are tiny particles of snow falling which give wonderful and weird effects with the sunlight shining through them -- they become coloured as well, as they fall to the ground in the still, windless air. My still shadow appears moving because of the tiny snow particles that come down. I shall never forget that experience. I'm sure it could be repeated, but it struck me then how heavenly it was and to encourage me."

On the 30th: "Returned to Lake Harbour and how lovely Rice Krispies taste!"

My "Dog Team"

I myself had been given two or three dogs, because I had hoped to be able to have my own dog team, especially thinking of the late Canon Turner, who went everywhere with his own dog team. But it wasn't easy. I kept at it for a year trying to build "my team" up. My first dog was called Qisseegeegitsiak. It's a long word which I made up – not very appropriately! – which would mean "a fine coat of [seal] fur." That's a long one shouting at him. And then the second dog I had was Qutchu – it meant a sort of white fur dog. The third one was Pinguat – which meant "the third one." The fourth I called "Sittamangat" (the fourth). So I only got as far as four dogs!

My first young dog – Qisseegeegitsiak!

Four hungry, Husky dogs – they take a lot of feeding! I must've been given food for my dogs – I didn't go hunting myself for food for them. The dogs and I relied upon local people's help. Some would bring a whole seal for me to cut up, store and freeze the meat into portions to feed my dogs with later on. I had to learn how to hitch a team up, and tie them up when not working. I also had to learn about making and sewing their harnesses, getting sealskin lines that attach from the harness to the qamutiik. Lots for me to learn!

A dog team is no romantic thing. It's hard to get them pull

together, especially when you don't have a proper leader. Dog teams do have to have a leader, and it's usually an older dog who can keep the younger ones in check. I didn't have such a dog! I saw kids with one dog, driving a little qamutiik around the community, and that was much easier to do with just one dog, compared with controlling four dogs. I eventually did learn how to hitch up the four of them, but that wasn't the end of the story. You have to teach them a way to go along on the sea ice, to give commands like telling the dogs to veer to the left. In Kimmirut it would be a command like "hurra, hurra, hurra" or to go right "ouk, ouk, ouk." They would learn these words and you would hope that they would obey your orders. I also had a great big, long whip to try and snap at them if they didn't do the right thing: also I would hurl the whip end at any of my four who were too lazy to go ahead and pull, or who tried to go off in their own direction. That happened too many times!

Dog teams going to the floe edge to hunt seals

So I learnt to eventually better control my small team, but I never really got very far with it. I felt that it was taking away from what I went there for. I wanted to study the language, and I wanted to be able to even do a sort of Bible correspondence course on Christianity for Inuit in their isolated camps. Then I also needed to have teaching material for children. That's what I wanted to do and was starting to do, but I didn't finish in the first year doing all I wanted. I had another matter on my mind!

Long-Distance Courting

You can guess what the "other matter on my mind" was. It was about getting married to my wonderful bride to be!

Margaret's letters had arrived safely after the Christmas mail drop. However, we didn't just rely upon the mail to communicate with each other; we also relied upon what was called the "single side-band" or SSB. The Hudson's Bay Company had radio communication with Pangnirtung, on a special frequency. That meant that there would be a spot on the radio whereby you could talk to each other when the conditions were right. Other people would listen into this SSB to try and catch the local news from other communities. So Margaret and I had arranged for a "sched" (scheduled radio call) every week whilst we were parted, she in Pangnirtung and me in Kimmirut. We'd talk away and just plan our wedding and wonder how it was going to go, and the various things that young couples want to talk about – although more subdued then, compared with how it would have been today!

We did this every week until it was nearly time for me to leave Kimmirut and Margaret to leave Pangnirtung to meet together in Iqaluit, to get married there. On our last "date" over the SSB I had to say, "Sorry folks, but this is the last time we'll by talking by SSB," and then people who had been listening to our courting over the radio, piped in and said, "No, we want you to carry on. We enjoy your talks!" So everyone was listening to what we'd been saying over the past year!

My Disastrous Fishing Expedition

After I had got home and recovered from my visit to Mingeriak's camp, I went to visit local camps by dog team. I also went, occasionally, hunting with Inuit, with their dog teams, or I would go on my own, looking for ptarmigan or rabbits. In those days there were no caribou around within easy travelling distance. Not many now either! In the fifties, however, there were many more caribou on Baffin Island than now, but they also made a large migration pattern on Baffin. At that time they were mostly north of us and were away from Kimmirut, which gave the impression of them being very scarce to hunt locally.

The next thing I can clearly remember is going with someone called Qaojakalo. He and his family were going fishing and I went with them. We went by dog team and it must've been early June. The trail they were using was going to a lake on the south coast of Baffin Island about 20 miles away from Kimmirut. To get there you had to go along a narrow shelf of ice that sloped down towards the sea and I thought, "It'd be easy just to slide right down that slippery ice shelf and go right into the sea!" But we managed all right and eventually arrived at the lake, and set up tents there, because it was fairly warm on the land around the sheltered lake. Soon the guys wanted to go fishing by first getting onto that lake.

The ice had started to melt on the lake and I felt scared to go too much on the lake, only safe where there was a real trail from people who'd walked to a certain place where there were holes in the ice, through which you could jig for the arctic char below. No one caught any fish whilst we were there for an hour or two. Would the guys give up? No way!! Instead, the guys wanted to try another fishing spot, having to walk over a fast-melting trail. I did not like the look of this watery trail, so I decided to not go with the guys and be safe. They went off and left me on my own. I thought, "Well I'll explore a little here." I started walking along the ice, taking great care to keep only to that which looked safe. I had my rifle slung on my back with a rope halter under my neck. Suddenly the "safe ice" I was on completely collapsed under me. It was candle ice! That meant that I went right into the water between the solid ice pans. Luckily the rifle didn't sink as it rested onto two bits of floating ice, the barrel on one piece and the butt on another piece! So it didn't sink, but me, I had to swim for it in this ice cold water in the lake, with no one around!

By the grace of God – and I'm sure my Guardian Angel was there to help me! – I finally got to what was a sort of safe ice spot, after swimming for a minute or so. I heaved myself up onto the proper ice, soaking wet, and made it to the lake edge where the tents had been pitched. I had to get back to our tent and look for some sort of towel to get dry with, and then get into my sleeping bag – but boy I felt cold after that! The weather had turned to be misty and cold, and I believe it was drizzling as well, after it had been quite a good day earlier. This all happened late evening near midnight – time doesn't matter when you have 24 hours daylight! I developed a heavy cold for a whole month after that adventure.

The guys eventually came back, and as far as I remember, they had caught fish. There I was – with none! I should have followed the Elders' advice and had gone with them. I had thought I'd known better – big mistake! I should have known that they would go on a safe trail, because they would know which is good ice and which is candle ice. I was really green and had to learn. It took me a long time to get to know the ways to do the right things in the North, especially when it came to fishing on the

Plans and Travel To Our Wedding

The next event was the HBC's supply boat that would arrive in July, the *Rupertsland*, the one that brought me to Kimmirut the year before. This boat would come when the ice broke up and a boat could come right into Kimmirut and unload there. Also as far as I remember for that year, later on, the hospital boat, the *C.*

D. Howe, would arrive as well. Now it was going to be this *C. D. Howe* that would eventually go to Pangnirtung after a long, long journey. It went around the north coast of Québec first, then eventually it would land up in Fort Churchill. The Bishop had planned that when it was going from Fort Churchill to Resolute Bay, and finally carrying on to reach Pangnirtung (this would be somewhere in the beginning of September), that's when my fiancée, my beautiful wife-to-be, Margaret Joan Porter, would get on that boat and would sail to Iqaluit! Yes, we had to then prepare to go get married in Iqaluit. That is where the Bishop had planned to fly into from a base in the States, Iqaluit being part of the DEW Line. The Bishop had to get permission from the Americans. Yes, Americans! Not Canadians. He would marry us as soon as he had arrived.

The other half of the plan was of course that I would get to Iqaluit, but there was no supply boat that would take me – unless I had got on the *C. D. Howe* in July. If I did this, I would have to be on it all that summer until September, when it finally would have reached Iqaluit. It didn't work out that way. There was no scheduled government boat from Kimmirut to Iqaluit, so it meant chartering a local Peterhead boat. In summer the Inuit did have small boats with a little outboard engine. Only a few had an inboard for their boat. To travel safely from Kimmirut to Iqaluit meant that I had to go on a Peterhead boat with its inboard engine. The one I chose to go with was Mingeriak's older brother, Davidee, who was a Helper in the Church at Kimmirut. He later took the surname of Davidee, so he became known as Davidee Davidee. He would take me to Iqaluit, when the time came, to meet up with the *C.D. Howe* there.

A Peterhead boat loaded up

He and I got things together for what we thought would be a three- to five-day trip at the most, and set out on September 1 to Iqaluit to meet the *C. D. Howe* with its most precious cargo on it – Margaret Joan Porter!! Well, it meant lots of preparation. I don't remember how much the Bishop paid for the gas and things like that, but it seemed that we had a good stock of supplies of food and ammunition. So we got on this boat, went at the Peterhead boat speed and got out into the Hudson Strait. There of course we got the full effect of the high wind and storm, so we didn't go too far that first night. Instead we had to anchor in a safe harbour, not far from where we had started.

The next day, we hoped, would be better, but no, it wasn't really much better at all. It was still rough and we didn't get far the second day either. Likewise with the third day, the fourth day just crawling along, from one little harbour to another. We were dashing to the next harbour during a lull in the almost constant wind. The waves were too white-crested and too dangerous to go through. This continued to happen until we finally got to the far southeastern tip of Baffin Island. We were going to start out again on the Saturday night. It's an amazing place. You've got to sail around the point that leads into Frobisher Bay. You've got to be there when it's high tide and calm. There's a terrific surge of water in between tides, which would make it impossible to go over – deadly dangerous – unless you proceed at the right time when it is almost high tide. The right time came early Sunday morning.

The route from Kimmirut to Frobisher Bay

Very thankfully, our prayers were answered! It was a perfect calm sea as we were approaching Frobisher Bay. You didn't suddenly turn into the Bay from Hudson Strait, but had to proceed along an awe-inspiring stretch of water near to the very high mountainous coast. Then you would go around a big point of land and finally into Frobisher Bay itself. It was a Sunday, and I was so thankful it was a Sunday, because at that time, and maybe it's still true today, you would not hunt on a Sunday. This was a place where it was too far for most hunters to go, but a place where there are lots of seals and other sea mammals. A place where there is a dead-calm, oily-looking shiny surface – all of this is a hunter's paradise. But it was Sunday. No hunting on a Sunday! If it hadn't been a Sunday, we'd have been spending a lot of time hunting seals in that area, and be delayed even more in getting to my love. Amazing blessing for me that it was a Sunday when we were there – there were lots of seals around, but not one was taken! I was getting very anxious – already a week had passed and no way to communicate with Margaret or the *C.D. Howe*. No such thing in those days as a radio strong enough to do it, so it meant hurrying up as much as we could. Thankfully the flat calm continued all the way to Iqaluit – what a difference from the Hudson Strait.

We carried on quite a long way, not side-tracking for seals, and finding a safe harbour near the end of a long mountainous fiord on the south side of Frobisher Bay. I was soon sound asleep on my little bench in the forward part of the Peterhead boat. The next day we made it all the way to Iqaluit. It was usually windy there as well. I was wondering, "Is Margaret still waiting for me?" I hoped she was! I was getting excited and suddenly realized, "I've got to get myself ready, get myself shaved properly, washed in this little boat, and I'm going to meet my love just later on today after being apart for over a year." The feeling was amazing and I was so excited. I hoped at the same time that I would still be the same for her, because when people don't meet for over a year, you don't quite know how the other person has changed. But you trust the Lord that we still both loved each other and that it would work out.

Our Wedding Aboard the C.D. Howe

So it was toward the evening that we got finally, finally, to see the *C. D. Howe* in the distance. We got closer up to it, and then I could climb up the rope ladder and there she was waiting for me! It was great to see her, but I was nervous as to what she would be like and what she would think of me. Would we still fully love each other? The Police were there as well. One of them had said to Margaret during her long wait for me, "Well if he doesn't want you, I'll have you!" The Bishop was pacing around the boat, anxious because he had to get back on a certain plane. I arrived three days later than when I was supposed to be there for the wedding. He had to wait all that extra time, and Margaret as well, although to this very day Margaret and I can't agree whether it was three days or four days. I say three, she says four, so we leave it to your imagination as to who is right!

The next day we were actually married at 2 o'clock on September the 10th in a service there on the boat. There was no usable Church in Iqaluit in those days. I was dressed up in a suit and "dog collar." We didn't really know the people who were there. Margaret had got a bridesmaid, and a best man for me, who I met for the first time. Margaret was given away by Inspector Larsen of the RCMP. A kind person with a good sense of humour – he jokingly said "Boy! I wish I'd never given her away!" As we know, he was the first person to get through the Northwest Passage on the *St. Roche*. You can see his signature on our Marriage Certificate, as well as a picture of our wedding.

Our marriage certificate

Margaret's "Dad" Inspector H. Larsen, about to give her away

Signing the Register as Bishop Marsh looks on

We were well guarded!

Davidee, his wife Mary and family, who brought me to Frobisher Bay

After the wedding, they thought that it would be a treat for us to go and look around Iqaluit. We went onto shore from the boat on a $1 million-barge! It was an amphibian, so could go onto the land as well. I said, "Boy! This is a slow old thing!" not realizing the cost of it. Anyhow, it got us to shore, and some people had arranged for us to visit a special USAF site on the DEW Line in Iqaluit, so we could see inside this dome-structured building. So we went to the "Dome," as it was called. Very secret place. People later on said they envied us being able to go inside the Dome. Very few, if any, locals were allowed inside there. But this was our wedding day treat!

We went inside, and I believe it was just a sort of radar indication of where various planes were in the sky. These positions were projected onto the high inner ceiling of the Dome. I didn't take much notice of it all, although it was supposed to be a special event for Margaret and me. I only had eyes on somebody – and you can guess who that was: Margaret Joan Porter. Now Mrs. Margaret Joan Gardener!

My wonderful bride Margaret Joan!

We stayed in a *C. D. Howe* cabin for our first night. After that, it was not clear where we were going to stay and we hadn't got a place booked for us. In those days, there was no hotel to stay in. It was only later on you got hotels in Iqaluit. So it happened that a person from the Department of Northern Affairs, as it was then called, Frank Allard, heard of our plight. He seemed to come out of nowhere in his car, stopped by us as we were wondering where to go, and said, "Come and stay with us!" We didn't need any coaxing to say "Yes please!" and got into his car. I guess he had a government car to use. He took us back to his wife Madge. Both of them lived in Apex, which is a small residential community three miles away from Iqaluit. They lived in a small house called a "512" (because it had an area of only 16 by 32 feet). When Frank got to Apex and we went in the house, Madge didn't say: "What are you doing with these two weirdos?" She agreed at once for us to stay there in their small house. Our first honeymoon was thus spent in Apex! Our second honeymoon came many years later in 1997, when Margaret and I went to the

UK. It was a small house in Apex, crowded with their effects, but they were kind enough to give us one bedroom in that house of theirs and to feed us. We were there for a day or two and then we were supposed to go back by helicopter to Kimmirut. We did go on the helicopter – it made two attempts to get to Kimmirut, but had to turn back both times because of the rotors icing up.

Before getting on to the helicopter, we couldn't bring any of our baggage, because it was all on the Peterhead boat. The weather had turned foul, so we both decided we would not go back to Kimmirut on that Peterhead boat, plunging up and down on some very rough seas. That would have been a real test of our marriage! Margaret's big trunk had got put on to Davidee's boat, assuming that we were going back to Kimmirut on his boat. It kept on being too rough to even go and fetch Margaret's trunk from the anchored boat. The Bishop had, in the meantime, got an offer from General Knap of the USAF to get us back to Kimmirut on one of their helicopters stationed in Iqaluit. It would be called "Operation Honeymoon!" That was the plan. After the second attempt we were beginning to wonder. But on the third attempt it was successful. That was about eight or nine days after we were married. I remember that amongst the very few personal things we could take on the helicopter with us, were these two items: a book called *Beyond Anxiety* and Eaton's catalogue!

I was very thankful when we finally made it to Kimmirut.

Our "Operation Honeymoon" USAF helicopter

Margaret's Arrival in Kimmirut

I don't know what Margaret really thought of our "new" first home together. It was built in 1944. Margaret settled down very well, fitting into the life there, and getting to know the people in Kimmirut, who very much welcomed her. It so happened that the *Rupertsland* was still there unloading supplies, so many Inuit had also come there to trade and help with the unloading of supplies. I had talked previously to Margaret about our house that we would be living in. She accepted the living conditions very well in spite of the lack of modern amenities and fresh food. One person who especially helped her settle in was Bess Parsons, the nurse stationed there. The two became great friends. It was also so convenient that they could visit each other, as our houses were so close together. Bess was married to the RCMP Constable, Bill. Even happily married ladies need another woman to talk with in addition to the husband!

Margaret and Ann, showing the Nursing Station in the background
(where our daughter Sue was born)

During the summer and fall there were quite a few people – around 300 – living in Kimmirut for Margaret and me to get to know. There were the boat builders, discussed earlier, who were building boats for the HBC – that was an interesting project to get employment for some local Inuit! The boat builders lived there with their families. They would eventually return to their hunting camps in the late fall. Then there were the more permanent residents of Kimmirut, as I previously mentioned. There were quite a few people to get to know as I counted everyone there as a parishioner. All except the permanent residents of Kimmirut lived in their tents during the summertime, and somehow still survived in them into the cool fall. All the tents had different coloured doors, because the RCMP had lots of different coloured paints left over, which they donated to the tent residents to paint their doors.

As September progressed it got to be colder, and then people would go back to their small isolated camps – this left very few people in Kimmirut.

Early Marriage Days in Kimmirut

After we had got back from Iqaluit on Operation Honeymoon, Margaret and I started our new life together. Neither of us had ever lived together in a home with just the two of us. It was going to be some adjusting to do! We were living in a different environment from what we were used to.

Two willing helpers - Margaret and Esther (the nurse there after Bess had left)

I had the wrong idea to start our married life together about which of us does things. I had the old-fashioned idea that a woman deals with all the *inside* of a house: cooking, cleaning, washing, everything, and the man deals with everything *out-side* of the house. Also, the man sees to all the finances. I would get the coal in for the coal fire in the kitchen. I would bring big snow blocks in for our washing water, which were put into a big 45-gallon drum by the kitchen stove, and so would eventually melt down – a large block of snow would not produce much water when melted! So you have to keep putting blocks of snow into the barrel to get enough water for washing dishes, etc. There was also a 10-gallon drum that was used for drinking water from melted ice. We didn't get the ice right in the actual small community. We had to go to a lake to cut the ice blocks in the fall when the thickness was just right. We cut the ice with four-foot long saws, which had a handle at one end. Then we had tongs to extract the ice blocks from the lake as we cut each one off with our ice saw. Then you would use these tongs to drag each block to a flat storage place, leaving each block upturned and accessible to easily collect it when needed. You can see our winter's supply in the background of the previous picture.

Me cutting our winter's supply of ice blocks.

Throughout the winter you would go and fetch them as you needed them, several at a time. Each household would do the same, so they would have the various groups of ice blocks ready to be used for drinking water. As you needed them they'd be put on the qamutiik and then you had to get them down to your home, then place them on a long plank of wood put between two oil drums. This "shelf" for the ice would be left just close to your outside door entrance Then you would just take them into the house as you needed ice water. But first with an ice pick, chip the ice into small bits before placing into the 10-gallon drum. Then you would hope that they would melt sufficiently for you to get a well-needed drink!

Delivering the cut up ice blocks (in 1965)

That lake is no longer there. There is now an airstrip where the lake used to be. There was no such "luxury" then as an airstrip. If we wanted to get on a plane, we had to either do it in summer when it could land on the sea water on floats, or wait for mid-winter when it could land on the sea ice with skis. Either way, when we were there it was only usually a single-engine Twin Otter RCMP plane to bring some mail to people and supplies to the Police.

We were very careful in our use of water for drinking from the melted ice. To get water for washing, you would heat the water from melted snow, about five gallons of it, in a big copper container, put on to the coal-fired stove. That covered container was called in Inuktitut tunmiujujak, "like a footprint," because that was the shape of the actual copper container. Then when we got our snow melted down and the tunmiujujak on the stove heating up the water, Margaret and I would then get into the bathtub. Not together! But first she bathed, and then I later. After we got out of the bathtub, dried ourselves, put clothes on, then we would wash a few clothes in the water that we'd just used to wash ourselves in. When we had washed a few clothes, we'd use that water to wash the floor. I have got a nasty feeling that it was Margaret who washed the floor while I did the collecting of the water and things like that – sorry!!

It was only after two years that we got a real washing machine. It was run off a small gas-powered generator. First you had to go the old way of melting the snow and getting the water hot enough in the tunmiujujak container, perched on top of the coal-fired kitchen range. Then put the dirty clothes and hot water manually into the washing machine tub. Hope the generator would start to power the machine and so do the laundry. A pulley system turned the agitator in the tub, as well as the hand-fed wringer sitting on top of the machine. When done and each item wrung out through the wringer, then hang the various clothes up to dry. This would be by hanging them up in the kitchen on a line or on a kitchen rack. It was a sort of pulley construction affair which made the wooden slats of the rack go up and down above the cooking stove in the small kitchen – congestion! After we had had our first two daughters, there was quite a to-do when we had to put the washed diapers on that rack to dry as well. In winter, if you tried to put things outside, they would go hard and solid straightway, so you couldn't do that. When I had to be away visiting camps it must have been really hard for Margaret to have to do all of this on her own!

Margaret had to make all of our own bread. She couldn't buy it at the store; also she had to bake cookies. She had to make our meals up more or less from scratch, using canned or dried goods. There was no freezer for us to use, except our cold porch when it was cold enough. Some people had tried to make a cold storage place in the ground for when the weather warmed up, but we didn't use that for a long time, because it really didn't do the trick, and we didn't have much to freeze. You had to have some good meat to freeze before you used that place in the ground!

From time to time some people from nearby camps would come in to trade. When they came in to trade, we entertained them and talked about their life there and ask about any way we could help or give them food or supplies they might need. Only at ship time and at Christmas did we really have many visitors from outside of the community. In the fall of 1956, we had several nurses and a cook off the *C. D. Howe* who came to visit us. They were on their way returning to Pangnirtung Mission Hospital. The cook was called "Willy" or "Kukuluk" – meaning, "dear loving cook." She really was true to her name! Kukuluk was the one Margaret had replaced in 1955-56 for the year that Kukuluk was on holiday. It was only because she was coming back to Pangnirtung after one year away that it was possible for Margaret to leave there and move to Kimmirut. You can imagine the welcome we gave her, knowing that she made it possible for us to get married after "only" one year apart, instead of the original plan of two years.

When there were no outside visitors, we would visit each other in the community. Often the RCMP guys would come to our house for coffee and a doughnut that Margaret had made. It was good to see them, and also they were able to get out of their "Barracks" situated on the opposite side of the fiord. They would write in their record book: "Went on Patrol to the Gardeners."

At Halloween, we would all play tricks on each other. I would go over to the Police living quarters and put a bucket of water on top of an open door somewhere in their house. In the meantime they would have taken our "honey bucket" (the pail inside a container that we used as a toilet) and put it up on the top of our Wind Charger platform, 30 feet up from the ground. We just wanted to have fun and play a joke on each other; that was the comradeship spirit we all had in those days, which could not be repeated today!

I felt that I had to be more part of the Inuit culture and not be like some outsider who would just observe people and then go away. One way to do this, I thought, would be, as I mentioned before, to have my own dog team. But they wouldn't go where they were told. There was no real leader and here's me learning to hitch up the dogs, put harnesses on them, getting them put into a fan hitch, bearded seal skin lines spread out, and starting to put each dog into his or her place, attached to one of the four extended lines, which were also attached to the qamutiik. Then off we'd go from the shore ice through the barrier ice and down onto the main sea ice.

One day as I was on the qamutiik and going along the trail, I had my hand and fingers around the outside of the qamutiik's runner. The runner went up against a solid lump of ice and then there was my finger stuck in between the qamutiik and an immoveable big block of barrier ice. My hand got squashed, but nothing broken, except my wedding ring on my finger. That did get squashed from round to oblong! Better, I guess, the ring than my finger. After this, my wedding ring was loose on my finger. Eventually, after we had moved to Kinngait (Cape Dorset), that wedding ring fell off, and is somewhere there in the rocks around the entrance to the old Community Hall. So to this day, the saying "There's gold in them thar hills" is true – the old Community Hall was built on top of a hill and that ring has never been found!

I should tell you another story about the Police that we knew while we were in Kimmirut, after the Parsons and the Barrs had left Kimmirut. They made home brew. Yeah, they made home brew in Kimmirut! There were two Police guys; one day there was a Police plane that landed and the two who were making homebrew saw a red serge uniform come out of the plane --an unannounced inspection! Here they were with this homebrew going on in one of their warehouses. I shall call the senior RCMP constable John and the other one Jack. John said to Jack, "I will go and keep those inspectors looking around the site while you go and hide the homebrew." John went and kept the Inspectors talking away and looking at little things, how the dogs are tied up, the names of their dogs and the state of the house, inside and everything, avoiding of course, the one warehouse where the homebrew was tucked away by Jack. But by the time John and the inspectors got to that warehouse, Jack had put all the cans right in front of the homebrew so you couldn't see it. To this day the inspectors never knew about that homebrew!

Our Day School

After I had settled down to life in Kimmirut, a job I had was to teach day school. There was no teacher there in Kimmirut. The federal government (who we called "the Feds") paid the Diocese for me to teach school, 50 cents per day per pupil. I think the Diocese gave us 50% of the final proceeds! The Feds also provided porridge and vitamin-enriched biscuits for the kids, as well as for myself. These biscuits were hard and very dry and uninteresting. The Feds provided textbooks, mainly Dick and Jane, and elementary math books and similar things. I would take the kids outside and around for nature and botany study – we'd do this mainly in the summer. But really sometimes it was me they took around! I would often have gotten lost, had it not been for them telling me the way. One time when a fog came down, as we were trekking along a winding valley, it seemed that we had lost all sense of direction. We only got safely back because some of the kids I had taken out were able to navigate back through the fog to Kimmirut.

Then I wanted to show the kids about how things are grown, so I got them to sow a few lettuce seeds to show this. When the *C. D. Howe* came that summer in 1956, a school inspector was on it and came to our "classroom" and said, "Oh that's great! You're teaching horticulture to the kids!"

Visiting Kinngait and Beyond

Between '55 and '57 I spent time trying to continue to learn the language. Being with kids and people and visiting them helped me a lot in grasping the basics of the Inuktitut language. I had also appealed for Sunday School materials from Scripture Press. They were wonderful and gave me lots of pictures and teaching material. I could then use them to teach the children many Bible stories and what they meant today. I got nothing from the Anglican Church!

Also I had a program where I would try to translate these stories to be given to people who came in to trade. I would also take them to give out when I visited camps. I thought that was a way to keep in touch with people. How do you really keep in touch with people spread out over 300 miles in scattered isolated camps? How do you keep them in the Christian faith? The answer lay in the fact that they did have their own New Testaments, Hymn Books and Prayer Books to use, which contained a lot more teaching materials than a usual Prayer Book in English. These books that they already had were a blessing, and made a real foundation on which to build up their Christian faith further. There was no need to have a Minister to be actually present, in order for them to be able to pray together or learn more. A camp leader would also do a lot to encourage people to do this and lead a little service week by week. I would thus have a congregation already there to continue to teach – also I would especially encourage and help the various camp leaders. My Scripture Press pictures would then be a good added bonus, especially for the children in the camp.

Then the time came for me to go beyond visiting just local camps for the day from Kimmirut. This happened when I knew that I had also to go to Cape Dorset (now called Kinngait), because there was no resident Minister stationed there. My four "little dogs" would never pull me all that way, so I had to find someone to take me there. They would have a "big reward" of 75 cents a day from the Diocese, plus payment of 50 cents for each sack of cut-up meat for dog food. The person I hired from a local camp was called Judai. He would take me to a camp which would be about 60 miles west of Kimmirut, pick up another guide to take me further on, whilst he would return to his home camp. My new guide was called Kooyoo and he lived in a camp called Taksirktok (meaning "foggy place"). He would take me to a third camp and then someone by the name of Peter would take me to a camp near Kinngait, to a place called Ikirassak (a place by a narrow strait of water going between two land masses).

The people in Taksirktok camp

When I got to Ikirassak, the camp boss/leader was called Pootoogook and he had quite a set-up, using a gas-powered generator for lights. He also used wind power as well. It seemed as if I'd got to Montréal – civilization! The house that I went to seemed to be really luxurious. Pootoogook was indeed a real leader, with many people who relied upon him for food. He had various servants. I went back to that house after it was no longer used, 20 years later. It had all fallen in and there was nothing there except the framework – it looked so small!

I don't think I felt nervous about getting ready to go to Kinngait and carrying on a hundred miles north to a place called Cape Dorchester. I had my two guides lined up with their two dog teams. Before I went I had to prepare a lot of things, especially to make a big bean stew. It was rather like the stew given out at Christmas time to the Inuit in the Church. My stew was made up in a big tunmiujujak, and as you might guess, made with a basis of dried beans, soaked then cooked, then adding whatever we had – canned corned beef, dried onions, dried celery, dried carrots and cans of tomatoes, plus spices, all cooked up together and then put in our porch to freeze. We had a porch attached to the Mission House that was not heated, so we could pour this bean stew out on to trays. Then I would divide the stew on the trays to make about 10-by-6 inch portions. Then, without breaking them up, I would put these frozen blocks of bean stew into pillowcases, to use as containers, to take them with us. We didn't have any plastic bags or proper food containers, so pillowcases "fitted the bill." I had to think of feeding my guide, and maybe a helper, when we were not in a camp. I also brought some hard candy along and cod liver oil pills.

My portioned out bean stew – ready for the trail!

I found it a problem, when in a camp, that we had this food, as we couldn't really share it with people. We had to have a reserve of enough food for many days of travelling ahead of us, when we weren't in a camp at all. Looking back, I'm surprised we didn't take with us more seal meat to have. Maybe my travelling companions were embarrassed to have to eat seal meat while I was around. Or maybe they felt (quite rightly so!) that because they're doing it for the Mission, that we'd be responsible for food. But the bottom line was that we had to have this frozen bean stew to have in our igluvigaq (overnight snow house – what people think of as "igloos") whilst travelling between camps. We did not want to rely upon being fed seal meat by others. When overnighting, we would take the frozen portions out and put them in a fry pan on the Primus stove, heat them up and enjoy eating them. But we couldn't do it very much whilst with others around, because one pillowcase of frozen bean squares would soon be gulped down and we would have nothing left!

You see, it was a special problem in 1957, when there was real hunger around. I know that people in the camp would share any food they had. But we could not and did not want to trade upon their kindness. Also, in 1957 it would be more likely that they hardly had any food for themselves. I sidetrack to say that we knew someone in 1957 called Jamesee, who walked – it must have been a hundred miles – to get food at the HBC store in Kimmirut. He was half-starved, but went from his camp to Kimmirut to go and get help, because they were all starving. The reason they were starving was that people couldn't go hunting, as there was too much deep, soft snow. That deep, soft snow affected us also. It was terrible going. When you would try to sit on the qamutiik, when you got tired of having to walk beside it in the deep snow, you would find that the dogs would suddenly stop their slow trot and all look around at you as if to say: "What are you doing sitting down on this qamutiik when we're so tired pulling you?" So we couldn't sit on the qamutiik. We had to walk a long way if we had to get to the next camp!

Usually though, when there wasn't starvation, the people who we visited would give us tea and some very nice bannock, beautifully cooked over a qulliq.

The tea was quite something. It was usually brewed up with 20 tea bags or so, already used many times, but somehow each time that they were brewed up, it let a little more tea out of the bag! Then the tea was poured out into an enamel, rather chipped cup, and then we would drink it. In those days we had sugar with our tea and they also usually had sugar, but not always. They were very happy when we brought our sugar and they could have that – it was better than gold!

After we had got to our host for the night, and had our tea and bannock, various people would come in to visit. We would talk a bit, catch up on the news, get to know any problems, find out any who were qammaq-bound to need a visit for prayer. Next we would have a short service in the jam-packed qammaq. I always prayed that there would be someone to lead the singing as the Lord has not given me that gift. I will wait until I can join the heavenly choir before I can lead singing! I felt very unworthy about that part of the work, but the Lord provided, because it always seemed that someone there knew the hymns, especially the ladies!

Part of my congregation in another camp

So after a long day out travelling, rather tired, I'd hit the sack and try to get refreshed for the morning. Usually all went to bed at the same time together – except there might be a young child sleeping before we did. The whole family would get onto the sleeping platform, more or less at the same time. Then there would be caribou skins laid out and we would put our sleeping bags on top of those, or some people just had some sort of blanket, sheet or caribou skin over them, without having an actual sleeping bag. Usually I heard nothing more once I'd hit the sack.

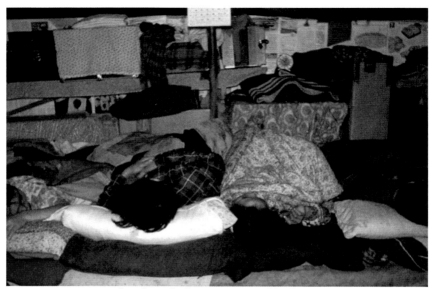

A sleeping platform at Qeeyookjuak camp

I did not have to even wait for the portable "pee can" which was discreetly passed around when we had just laid down on the sleeping platform. Before hitting the sack I would have quickly gone outside to pee there, hoping that's all I'd have to do. If I wanted to do more, I would take a big stick and look for a big rock to go behind, always followed by a hungry dog. It was cold at times but I learnt how to be quick and deal with the situation!

Starting to build an igluvigaq – overnight snowtel!

When travelling, we would stop in the middle of nowhere on some island where the depth and hardness of the snow was just right. Judai was a good igluvigaq builder. This word means "a temporary snow house for overnight." Originally the word "iglu" (commonly spelled "igloo") meant a snow house that is resided in as a base – not just a temporary one for overnight. It took Judai or Kooyoo one hour or a bit less, if the snow was just right for building the igluvigaq. There was our "snowtel" for the night! Whilst he was building, I would chink the holes between the snow blocks with snow. Doing this got me warmer! I often felt quite cold in the feet and hands in spite of good warm clothing. The cold really made you hungry. This was really the only time I felt the cold unless there was a blizzard. We would not travel in a blizzard. We'd stay in the igluvigaq all day. I found this very relaxing and was glad to be able to do this. I was sorry that I had to do this for only one day in 1957. In later years there were not many occasions either, that we had to stay in an igluvigaq for the whole day.

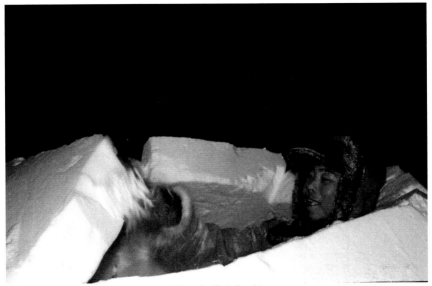

Nearly finished!

Snowtel completed

My first attempt!

When I visited isolated camps I would use a Prayer Book, Hymn Book and New Testament all written in syllabics. In those days every household had a copy of these books, and so it was easy to lead services and do some teaching, especially for the camp leaders who, every Sunday, would gather the rest of the people in the camp for worship and reading of the appointed daily Bible reading (from Scripture Union). Here is an example of one of my favourite verses, John 3:16, in Inuktitut: ᑏᒪᒃ ᑕᒃᕙ ᒍᑎᐅᑉ ᓯᓚᒃᔭᐊᕐᒥᐅᑉ ᓇᒃᓕᒋᕚᓪ ᐃᕐᓂᑐᐊᓂ ᑐᓂᖕᒪᒍ ᓇᓪᓕᐊᓪ ᑖᑦᓱᒧᖕᒐ ᐅᒃᐱᖅᑐᖅ ᐊᓯᐅᖅᑯᓇᒍ ᓅᖑᓱᐃᑦᑐᒥᒃᑕ ᐃᓅᓯᖅᑲᖅᑯᓪᓗᒍ. (For God so loved the world that he gave his one and only Son, that whoever believes in him shall not perish but have eternal life). There was a selection of about 150 hymns from which to choose. The Inuktitut Prayer Book also had extra teaching material in it, in a form something like a Catechism (illustrated below), in addition to the various services. We would go through some of this teaching and re-affirm the need of the Christian Gospel. Then in this Prayer Book there were daily morning and evening prayers for each day of the week, which each household would use. So my aim was to build up on what had already been done and not just "take a service."

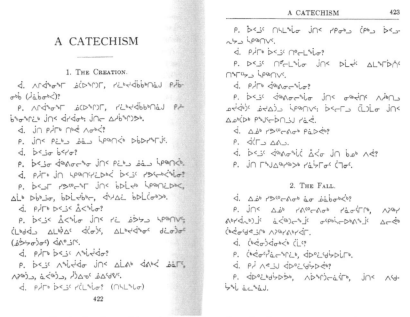

Part of a Catechism in Inuktitut (*Book of Common Prayer*)

At each camp I would still try to communicate in Inuktitut, as nearly all were monolingual. I really had prayed to the Lord to help me and I know He answered. In my talks I would use a visual aid from a company in the States that I had seen advertised. It was part of a series called "Sermons in Chemistry." This is what it was: I would have a blackish-looking solution to represent our transgressions, and then another solution, red, representing the blood of the Lord. When the red solution was added to the black solution, the latter would go clear. It was a very clear basic illustration upon which to build. It had to be clarified that this important step in our faith was fully understood, before going on to see how accepting this fact in our hearts produces so much blessing in our lives afterwards. To know we are forgiven sinners is the greatest gift we could ever have! This visual illustration and building up from it, I believe was the best way to get the Gospel message across. I have always been a believer in making our talks visual as much as possible, to be better remembered afterwards.

Then maybe, later on in the day when I was at a camp, I would take a Holy Communion service and maybe lead a Baptismal service, although I can't be sure whether I did this in 1957. I think it was really only in 1958, because I couldn't really do it sufficiently well to try and attempt it as soon as 1957. I'd also do any marriage preparation required. I would talk with the children using my Scripture Press pictures. In 1957, I found it very hard to do these things, but of course as I learned the language more, I found joy in leading these special services. It was especially a happy time when talking to the children and giving them some hard candy, which they treasured very much. That type of hard candy has still the same look that is sold in the stores today!

At times I took my piano accordion with me in its original red box that had come safely from England. I couldn't play by ear, so I had to use a hymn book with the music score. I played the accordion with my one finger to try and teach a new hymn. Margaret had helped me a lot in this, in getting to know the tune of a hymn. I'm glad that no one recorded my piano accordion "playing!"

So that was the routine. It happened again in 1958, 1959, and 1960. One time, during my 1959 visit to a camp with Kooyoo and his son, Eyeetseak, we were on the sea ice trying to go to a camp and a blizzard developed. We all seemed to have lost sense of direction, going around in circles. We were scared that we might be heading out to where there was open water or dangerous ice without knowing it, because of the white-out conditions. Kooyoo decided that we should stop where we were and build an igluvigaq there and then, even with great difficulty. The igluvigaq building material is very poor on newish ice. Anyhow, an igluvigaq was finally built! We did our usual routine of unloading supplies from the qamutiik, and securing everything away from the dogs – they would chew the whole lot if we left them too easily accessible. We put furs, the Primus stove, food, kettle, etc. into the igluvigaq. Kooyoo always brought along a gasoline pressured lantern for light, as well as a Primus stove for cooking. In those days there was no Coleman stove; it was a Primus stove. He also brought along a qulliq and some seal blubber just in case we needed it for heat and light. He also brought spare kerosene for the Primus stove. So it's amazing how well I was looked after, and how the Lord was behind all of this, to make it possible to be physically fit enough to travel in these conditions.

Well, you can imagine all these supplies to be unloaded and stored after building the igluvigaq, and the effort that was needed to do this. The next morning, when we woke up and looked outside, the blizzard had stopped. There, right ahead of us, about 100 yards away, we saw the camp we were heading to. All that work we did to camp out overnight was for nothing! We had a good laugh about all of this.

Inside the newly built igluvigaq

When we were nearing Kinngait, we stayed at the camp whose leader was Pootoogook. He was a very smart man with various servants. He had a wife called Ningeokuluk and had five sons, although one of the five had died by 1957 with tuberculosis. He was supposed to be the leader to succeed him. Pootoogook was really quite powerful. He would not let his servants buy what they wanted when they all went into trade at the store, unless he okayed it, after he, Pootoogook, had done his trading first. He also gave orders out by signs. As an example, I'm not sure of the exact finger, but one finger raised would mean "bring me tea or coffee." Two fingers meant "bring me a cigarette." Three fingers, "Bring me some food." Four fingers, "Bring me my parka." However, in spite of his autocratic ways, the Lord used him to feed a lot of people, by providing them with food when they would have otherwise starved to death, because they did not have the right equipment for hunting. Pootoogook and a few others in the 1930s had got very rich by trapping foxes. Because white fox furs were then selling at a premium and he had sufficient servants to trap many foxes, he collected enough money to buy a good boat and hunting equipment. He was thus able to help feed many people who otherwise might have starved to death. We also have to thank Pootoogook that there was a beautiful little Church already built in Kinngait before I ever went there. It was Pootoogook who pursued his aim to have this Church built under his leadership. I must add that I had a little battle concerning the name of this Church. It was to be called St. Augustine's – a foreign name to most Inuit. I was able to get the Diocese to rename it St. John's.

St. John's Church, Kinngait, with parishioners outside

When I got to Pootoogook's camp, Kooyoo would return to his camp and I would have a fresh team of dogs driven by Pootoogook's son called Paolassie. He would take me to Kinngait for a stop-over there, staying in the HBC Manager's house in Kinngait. Bill Hall and his wife Helen were a very kind couple. I would have a bath there – and I sure needed it! I was made extremely welcome. In fact, I think I got so spoiled that I hardly wanted to move out. Helen always made me feel at home and she made a beautiful salad using her dehydrated cabbage flakes. I wonder if it would seem so nice to have now. How glorious it was to sleep in a bed, to have a cooked meal put before me. Then some rest, relaxation and talking to Margaret by the SSB to find out how she was getting on. I was worried about her being on her own. Thankfully though, she managed very well by herself!

Then I'd go on to Cape Dorchester over some very high, yet flat and windy terrain. I think we almost got lost going over this great flattish plateau, because there were no landmarks. There was nothing in the way of a landmark that I could see as to which way you went. Somehow Paolassie knew what to look for, by looking at the direction of the snow ridges that had been left by past blizzards – these would direct him to the right way. We prayed every night for guidance to get safely to where we were going.

We finally arrived at Cape Dorchester and stayed there two or three days. We were given lots of frozen walrus meat. I found it good and juicy. Somehow it was a very mild meat – just like beef. Not as strong as seal meat. I often say that my teeth were worn down by chewing a lot of frozen walrus meat! The leader of that camp was called Manomee – he was a great carver and art-ist. So after I stayed there, visiting the people, taking services and doing what was necessary to be done, we went back again to Kinngait. From there we revisited all the camps that we had been to on our outward journey. I think it was about six weeks that I was away and all this time Margaret was on her own. That was in 1959, when she was pregnant with Sue, and had by that time Ann to look after! I arrived back that year on April 1. She had got worried about my long absence with no means of com-munication. The next day the Police were going to search for me. I got back home just in time!

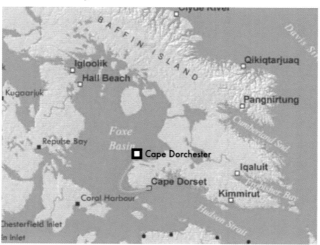

I'm sure it was only by the prayers of others that Margaret survived. I think I had got someone to help her bring in snow and ice, also coal for our stoves. While I was away, I know she sometimes had to go outside to get coal to stoke up the two stoves in our house. She also had to welcome visitors from camps, get them something to snack on and tea to drink, when they came in to the visitors' room to visit. She was very pregnant all of this time! Of course there was the nurse nearby, as well as the Hudson Bay, so she did have a place to visit. Margaret thought I'd be coming back within a week or so, after I had talked to her on the SSB through the Hudson Bay radio in Kinngait. We never reckoned on the deep snow! When I finally got back to the Mission House and settled in again she had prepared supper. She had made up a salad from the dehydrated cabbage and other ingredients that we had. Then to my shame and embarrassment now, I said to her, "I really like the salad that Helen Hall makes – you should get the recipe." I'll never live that down!

Medical Rescue By RCMP Plane

To go back a little in time to 1957, in the fall of that year Margaret had got pregnant and soon got the typical morning sicknesses and didn't seem well – then she started bleeding. She talked to the doctor about it and he said she should go to Iqaluit for a D & C. This was easier said than done. It was the fall. You couldn't get a plane to land on the sea because it was too cold for the plane to land on floats and not thick enough ice to support the weight of a plane on skis. I was worried about her. We could only pray for a way to be made to deal with the bleeding.

Eventually, however, an RCMP plane was sent from Iqaluit to "medevac" her (medical evacuation by airplane). I believe the Police guys in Kimmirut, Bill Parsons and Cliff Barr, consulted with the Inuit and said a plane should be able to land on the lake near Kimmirut. The ice there would've been thicker than the sea ice; being freshwater ice it would freeze sooner at a higher temperature. So a plane was sent, but it was such a wind Margaret and I could only just make it to the lake. On the lake we could hardly stand up because the wind blew you down. But by a miracle and a wonderful pilot, Lorne Fletcher, the plane somehow managed to land in the gale force wind on sheer ice. I truly was blown along by the wind on the clear slippery ice. Margaret somehow got on to that plane and went to Iqaluit, where they also had another scary time trying to land in a gale-force crosswind. There was no hospital in Iqaluit at that time, only a Nursing Station, where she was taken. There was, however, a doctor there. This doctor was about to do a D & C when he said, "You have a living fetus in there!" The only answer to this was that Margaret had twins, but one was lost. How deeply thankful I was that she was safe, and we could still have our wonderful first baby, Ann Symata.

Margaret had to go South for Ann's birth because of the potential difficulties for a safe delivery. She stayed near Toronto with a very kind Church family, Elsie and Harold Stephenson. They made her very welcome. How thankful we feel to them who lovingly looked after Margaret and made her part of their family.

Margaret's Return Home with Baby Ann

Margaret came back to Kimmirut the next year on June 30, 1958, with our little first-born daughter, Ann Symata. She was only 4 pounds 7 ounces. She weighed less than a bag of sugar! Margaret and she came back on the *C. D. Howe*. Some people were very doubtful whether a mother should have a tiny babe like that on a boat going to the Arctic. But Margaret was brave and said, "I'm going home!" Luckily that year there was not much ice, so the boat could come directly from Montréal to Kimmirut. Margaret could easily get from the *C. D. Howe* to the shore by the boat's small bubble-type helicopter. Home at last! What an answer to prayer! It was amazing to think how she was sent away sick in the fall, and thought she had had a miscarriage – there she was coming back with our baby. To us, it was the working of the Lord and a miracle. We can only think that when she bled she must have lost one of her twins in the womb. And then it hit me, "Wow! I'm a dad!" It was a wonderful feeling.

We had only two bedrooms in that Mission House. Later on we put Ann in one bedroom and Margaret and I in the other. As far as I remember we had got some sort of crib and baby furniture for Ann, but I'm sure they were not very much compared to what people have today. It was a new experience to me. I don't think I realized how basic things were then. There was no way to go and warm up the bedrooms, because you're upstairs and the coal fire is downstairs – if it's still alight! It would have gone out some-times during the night. We prayed it wouldn't. When it did go out during the night, it was pretty cold in the whole house, and for a little tiny babe that was not the right thing. It would have been warmer in a qammaq, where the qulliq never goes out, as long as it is kept going with oil.

Our life changed, like anyone else's when there's a newborn in the family. We were sort of still newlyweds in our own little world, even after over two years into our married life together. However, our life changed to centre around Ann. It was a bless-ing to have a child who slept well and she could take milk from her mother. We still had to carry out our usual chores and routine, looking after the ice and water, and now dealing with dirty diapers! There was no such thing as disposable dia-pers. They were cloth diapers and they needed washing – quite a lot of them! There was only the melting snow by the stove to have enough water to wash them in. That was a challenge for me and for Margaret, but we managed. By that time we had got the "modern" gas-fired washing machine. We still had to dry the diapers after they'd been washed, using our pulley set-up over the kitchen range.

We also had to run the Day School that we held in our house. Margaret helped so much in that. We also had to entertain camp visitors when they came into trade, and I had to visit the Inuit to learn the language and customs, take services, and have our own prayer life.

There was one time in the summer of 1956 that was funny. I was trying to learn about the Inuit culture by being with Inuit as much as possible. On this particular day, I followed several Inuit to go visiting with them to various tents. That's what I had to do to learn the language and customs. However, this time, the people I'd followed didn't want me to go with them. Why? It was because they were going to go together to eat seal meat that was raw. They were shy of a non-Inuk going and seeing them cutting open a freshly caught seal and starting to eat all the bloody parts. In a tent, the people would gather around the seal, placed on a cardboard under-pad on the floor. The seal would then be cut open- the intestines, heart, liver etc. separated and then the main meat pieces cut off the body, giving the traditional women's cuts of meat to them. The women were usually chatting away in a little group of their own, to leave the men talking about hunting places and their experiences in catching the seal we would be eating. All would be chit-chatting and laughing away, gulping down the juicy bloody meat. In those days, the women ate certain parts and the men ate other parts of the seal. On this occasion, the people I was following tried to shake me off, but somehow it didn't get through to me what they were trying to do. They would sort of avoid going to where the feast was going to be, going to other tents instead, so that I wouldn't be with them at the feast and they wouldn't be embarrassed by me being with them. After a year or two, that all changed, and they realized that I could fully join in with them, so I was invited to many seal meat feasts. We all laughed at how they used to try and stop me going to feasts and now they were asking me to go!

I didn't mind raw seal meat. In fact I found it a necessity to keep my body warm and stoked up. Margaret didn't like it, because when she was in Pangnirtung Hospital as a cook, she had to cook so much of it, that it turned her off eating seal meat. Not an acquired taste for her!

Margaret and I were really happy in Kimmirut. We always look back upon it as maybe the happiest time we had as missionaries. It was, however, a hard situation for me to keep a good balance among learning the language, Church work and teaching, joining in feasts, going to Inuktitut country-style dancing, hunting with Inuit hunters, dealing with my little dog team, and also being able to devote my time to being with Margaret and Ann.

Scary Events and Safe Delivery of Baby Sue

Once when Ann was only two years old we had a scary time with her, as she suddenly got very sick. It was with some fever that made her almost lose consciousness. We didn't have a doctor to contact and there was no nurse there either. We could only pray. She did get better, again we believe only by the Lord's answer to our prayers.

Another time there was a lady who was completely crazy – almost, I would say, demon possessed. At times she had to have six guys to hold her down. There was a nurse in Kimmirut then, but she didn't know what to do. That was a time when I really felt the Lord's presence, when we could only pray for this lady, Mialisaa. She was completely healed by the Lord, and I can think of no other explanation at all. She continued to live a normal life, serving her Lord, her Church and her community until she died in 2018.

There was also a time that I shall never forget, when I had a very bad toothache and had to get the tooth out. There was no dentist in Kimmirut. The *C. D. Howe* had gone away long ago. I believe there was no nurse in Kimmirut at that time, but the Police were people who could take teeth out. But with this tooth, when they tried to take it out, I just couldn't bear the pain – it had twisted roots. So I had to be put to sleep by people who didn't know how to do it! Poor Margaret had to drop the anaesthetic right onto me, so I was right out of it. Whilst I was out of it, I must've vomited my breakfast up – to this day it's a miracle to me that it didn't kill me by choking me to death. I've known people who have been put on an anaesthetic who have vomited and died because of being suffocated. The tooth did eventually come out with its twisted and infected roots. The whole process took about three hours!

Sue was born the next year and she's the only one who was born in the North. It was different with Sue than with Ann, as Margaret was considered to have no possible complications for a safe delivery. There was also a nurse in Kimmirut at that time. Esther was a great nurse and she was willing to deliver the babe. All went very well.

Sue was safely delivered in that tiny little Nursing Station right by our Mission House! She was a bonnie 8 pounds 12 ounces. In those days, fathers were not allowed to be in the actual delivery room. Instead, I had to wait patiently outside of the Nursing Station – even if I had been allowed in, it would have been a very crowded room!

CHAPTER 3:
KINNGAIT

Exodus from Kimmirut and Proposed Move to Kinngait

During the summers of '57-'59, there was an exodus of people going by boat to Iqaluit. They had to go, packed in small freighter canoes, hugging the coast of South Baffin, around the Eastern tip of South Baffin and into Frobisher Bay. These people were going to Iqaluit for work because there wasn't much work in Kimmirut. The sealskin prices had dropped a lot, so people thought the only way was to go and get formal employment in Iqaluit. When I first arrived in Kimmirut, there were over 300 people. By 1959, there were only just over 100.

The Bishop said that this all meant that we would have to move to Kinngait. Kinngait had no Minister. In fact, there were just three Ministers on all of Baffin Island. So in the summer of 1960, I had to go to Kinngait. There I was, commissioned to get some workers together to start preparing a site in order to build a new Mission House. Me?! Previously, while I was still in Kimmirut, the Bishop had mailed me blueprints to study -- blueprints for the new Mission House to be. I always remember that when looking at the blueprints I said, "I wonder which way up they go?" Yes! You can guess I was pretty naive about house building. There was I, being told what I had to do to build the Mission House and get some workers to do it – I couldn't even read a blueprint!

In Kinngait, Jim Houston, in charge there for the Feds, was a great help to me. He helped me choose the right site for the Mission House to be. It was rather pre-set where it had to be, which was near the Church. Pootoogook had built the Church there quite a long way away from the main community settlement. It was in another valley that must have been half a mile away from the main community. This site being far from the main community seemed weird then, but he had real insight, as now so many houses have been built in that area, conveniently placed near the Church.

Building Our Kinngait Home

So there I was, never in my life before having even considered building a house. I did not know how to do it. Tried to get some ideas and read up about it, and then had to hire about eight workers to build the house. So I was sent there to Kinngait in the spring of 1960. I first had to stay in Iqaluit for several weeks waiting to hitch a ride on a plane going to Kinngait. I was put up by a kind person there called Vic Brown and his wife, until I could eventually get my ride. My stay there showed me the wild side then of Iqaluit, mainly because of drunkenness. Lots of people, especially at night, were running around very drunk, yelling and chasing people. We were able to hold some mission services and quite a few gave their lives to the Lord.

After safely arriving in Kinngait, I had first to build the foundation for the house. A lot of boulders and rocks were used to do this, all by manual labour. Most were quite heavy but moveable. With various crude instruments, workers piled the rocks on top of each other, so that we got a raised solid foundation. The foundation was at least four feet high on one half, and then petered down to less on the other side of the foundation. The whole foundation for the house would be about 60 feet in length and the width would be about 40. The house itself was 48 feet by 24feet. It was quite a big pad to build – that's a lot of rock to move and put into place! I believe I was allowed to credit each worker, who had laboured all day at doing this work, the princely sum of $2 per day!

Also in addition to the house pad, I had to build a large pad beside the Mission House for our lawn. That's what we wanted for the kids to be able to play on and to sit outside and have a picnic. We went out to the opposite island to get the Arctic turf, put the rolled-up turf into a freighter canoe, crossed back to our house, and then unrolled the turf to lay the rolls out onto the rock pad. All that work was worth it, as all looked quite nice after we had finished doing our project. We made a path around the house, and put gravel on it – the workers did a great job. Then we were ready for the actual building materials that would come off the cargo ship.

Pad and paths done, the cargo boat arrived and we started to build. Thanks to the Inuit, all I had to do was the measuring, planning what building materials would be needed day by day, and making them available. I had to keep eight workers occupied in a meaningful way. There I am, a real rookie, doing something I'd never done before, and yet trying to be in charge of much more knowledgeable Inuit workers than I!

Workers building the new Kinngait Mission House

The workers really worked well together building the new Mission House

We started to build and really it was going up very well. No power tools – everything done by hand. The whole framework went up without a hitch. Then after a few weeks I realized that we seemed to be running out of building materials. All the walls and the floor were done. Then when the walls and floor had been done, there was a terrible realization that there were no materials left for the roof! There were the interior plywood sheets, which were meant for a ceiling, but the plywood was an indoor type and not roof material. In my alarm I sent a telegram to the Bishop stating our dilemma. A few years later I was told by his Secretary, that when he heard the news he said, "If Mike Gardener wants a roof, he should order one!" I heard something similar about Dave Ellis, the one who accompanied me to Kimmirut from Chimo. When he got to his Mission Station in Salluit he found there were no nails for the whole house. He, of course, messaged the Bishop. The Archdeacon, Jamie Clarke, heard this and said "Faith is a poor substitute for nails!"

We had this Mission House to be erected that summer of 1960. We would have to leave it for the winter – unfinished! I could only leave it with interior-grade plywood covering the tops of the house walls as our only makeshift barrier against the rain and snow to come. We also did have some polyethylene to help out, but it was hard to keep the sheets laid out over the plywood, without blowing away. We really tried to make the house rainproof, but that summer was such a wet and windy one. It rained so much, cats and dogs. The water that still came through our paltry roof barriers was channelled into 45-gallon empty oil drums, which would then be emptied when getting full. In those days there were no "Sched" flights to bring in missing supplies, so you had to wait for next year's boat to put the missing and other materials on. There was nothing more that we could do other than taking time to get our temporary "roof" better sealed. Because of this, and because Margaret and I had not been on holiday for five years, we felt it best to take our holiday and visit our parents. I wonder who'd like to sign on to something for a five-year stint without a break today. But we didn't mind, because we felt so much at home in Kimmirut.

That was our Paradise. We really loved it there. We felt that Kinngait would be different, but eventually we also got to like very much being there in Kinngait.

Our finished Kinngait House

Going on Holiday to the UK

Margaret had gone on ahead from Kimmirut to England. She stayed in a house near Bognor, on the South Coast. I left Kinngait on an icebreaker in the fall to go to join her. I literally had to hitchhike to go south. Luckily for me, I could get out by the way of an icebreaker that had happened to anchor by Kinngait. It was on its way to Churchill. Nothing arranged by the Diocese. Looking back I don't know how I did it, boarding this icebreaker as a stranger to them. No red tape, no money or special documents needed! Try that today! And then I was able to get a ticket to Toronto from Churchill, but I still had no money. I don't know how it was, but I somehow or other got on the train at Churchill and was able to go to Toronto, and from there go to the Arctic office. They were able to arrange for me a passage on a boat over to England, and then I went to the house that Margaret had rented. We stayed there several weeks.

Yes, Margaret had already got to England. She left on the RCMP plane, which had flown from Kimmirut to Iqaluit. In Iqaluit, she got a Nordair DC8 propeller plane to Montréal. When in Montréal, she stayed with the Tincomes. The Tincomes were the most wonderful people you could meet. They really deserve to be recognized. Whenever missionaries would pass through Montréal, they were welcomed into their home, fed and watered, and they, the Tincomes, never received any recompense. Hal and Myrtle did all of this for the Lord. Also, besides having missionaries living in their house and taking them to stay in their country cottage for an extra holiday, they also visited Inuit patients regularly in the various hospitals in Montréal. They would take Inuit shopping, arrange for trips for them, fed them, and made them so welcome. I'm really hoping that they will be recognized more in the days and years to come. They had a great willingness to help, gave us such a welcome, understood some of our odd Northern ways, and had a vital interest in the Mission work of the Anglican Churches in the North. They wanted to do this and we'll be eternally thankful for all they did do.

Hal and Myrtle Tincombe with a friend (in the middle)

It was a good holiday in England, when I eventually had got there. At last I was able to be with Margaret and our two little girls Ann and Sue. Just imagine it, the time we were apart, and not a way to directly communicate until we actually met. I was able to go to where Margaret was, in a rented house near Bognor, and enjoy a little holiday by the sea. After this sea holiday, we went to stay with my parents in Egham. But it wasn't all holiday, as I had to do deputation work. Usually, once a week, I went around to various churches that were near Egham, to go and show slides that I'd taken whilst in Kimmirut and Kinngait. We had some problems in relationship issues with my father while we stayed at Woolston, so we moved to stay at the Foreign Mission Club in London. We spent our Christmas there in rather sparse surroundings. However, because we were considered to be missionaries, we got a very cheap rate for our stay. I am eternally thankful to the Foreign Missions Club for doing this in our time of need! My father had been taken to Chertsey Hospital with chest problems. He later died in that hospital on New Year's Day, 1961. We then had to deal with his estate and make funeral arrangements with the Church in Egham.

It was also on this so-called holiday I wanted to take a course about Christian education. So the four of us stayed in a rented house near St. Christopher's College in Blackheath. The Principal was a Miss Hardcastle. She might have had a "hard name" but she had a soft heart! We always remember one of the students, whose name was Mr. Peter Cargozzi. I know our kids were scared of him because he was a black person. In those days there were very few non-Caucasians around London, so somehow his "strangeness" scared our two. We did, however, have a good time, and learned a lot about making Sunday School interesting and appropriate for those who attend.

Mr. Peter Cargozzi, Miss Hardcastle, students and our family
at St. Christopher's

The Move to Kinngait

I don't remember exactly how we got back to the Mission House in Kimmirut, when our holiday time was over in England. I do know we went back by boat to Montréal and would have flown to Iqaluit from Montréal. There we would have waited for an RCMP plane, to hitch a ride on it back to Kimmirut. We stayed with Doug and Jean Dittrich in the Iqaluit Mission House. They were very kind to us and we enjoyed their hospitality and fellowship. We still enjoy keeping in touch with them after all these years.

We got back to Kimmirut in April and had to pack up items in the Mission House to be ready for the move to Kinngait. We had to wrap up each item in black tarred roofing paper, which was really used for insulation purposes. I believe we ended up having about a hundred pieces, but no heavy furniture. All these items had to be packed up ready to be sent to Kinngait, when the boat would come in the summer.

All packed up, ready to go to Kinngait

In the meantime, Bishop Marsh said he would need to order new furniture to replace the pieces we weren't taking to Kinngait. The new furniture would be going in the new Mission House in Kinngait, which had yet to be finished. He said to us, "Mike, let me know if the furniture you get from Hudson Bay Company, when it is off-loaded from the boat, if it is of poor quality." Well, we were happy that he said that, and when the furniture did arrive in Kinngait, the sofa and chairs were of terrible quality! I therefore wrote a letter to him, because he had asked me to do so, telling him this. I got a terrible letter back from him saying how ungrateful I was to not like the furniture he had sent in. He had forgotten his original request!

Next, I had to go to Kinngait to be there when the supply boat came with the materials for the Mission House roof, which had not been completed the previous year. Whilst waiting for the boat, I visited and got to know people, including Jim Houston, Terry Ryan, the famous artist Kenojuak and other very artistic people we have now heard about. Terry and I were billeted together in a small Transient Centre, because there were no hotels in those days. Terry and I became good friends and he and Jim eventually got a print shop going, employing several very talented artists. Kinngait original prints are very much sought after to this day. On my first visit to Kinngait by dog team from Kimmirut, when I was about to return to Kimmirut, Jim asked me if I wanted to buy any of those first prints for $40 each. I said "no thanks" – I could not see how I could get them back to Kimmirut on a qamutiik – let alone finding the money to pay for them. A missed golden opportunity!

After the supply boat had been through, a carpenter was sent by the Bishop to complete the house, the roof especially. I was so happy that there was a carpenter who could do it properly because I'd never built a roof in my life. If I had tried it would have been a rather leaky roof – or it would have been blown away in a blizzard! Anyhow, the house was soon finished. I was very thankful that there was no water damage from the previous year, with only the leaky, temporary, ceiling type of roof that had been left on over the winter of 1960.

Then I had to go back to Kimmirut where Margaret and our two daughters were waiting. I don't think then I realized how hard it was for Margaret, with all this coming and going, exact details of which I've forgotten to this day. There, we felt sad to have to pack up all our belongings and move to Kinngait. To get to Kinngait, we had to be all packed up and ready to go on the ice-breaker, the *CCGS N.B. McLean*. It was a hard time waiting, with two little ones, and to live day by day with all our things packed up.

To get to the icebreaker we had to board a small boat, because the *McLean* didn't drop anchor right in Kimmirut. Instead, it anchored out in the Straits about eight miles away. Margaret, Sue, Ann and I got into the small boat that the RCMP had kindly provided for us, and started out to get to the icebreaker. It so happened it was a very foggy night. Calm, thank goodness! So the four of us were taken out to try to find this boat whose exact location we did not know. Just imagine searching for it in the fog, in the middle of the night, with our two little ones feeling very cold. There didn't seem to be adequate communication in those days.

We finally did find it, but there was no proper gangway put down from the boat. Instead, we had to climb up a rope ladder hanging over the side of the boat. We had to get up it from our little boat, trying to do this in the dim light, and make it up to get onto the *McLean*'s deck. I don't recall who went up first, although I'm sure it must have been Margaret. We held Ann up, and then the Police held her and got a little way up the rope lad-der, until she was grabbed by some of the crew from above. Sue was in the hood of Margaret's amauti (a parka with a pouch at the back for carrying a child) – this little babe in her hood must have made Margaret feel as though she was falling backwards as she climbed the rope ladder. That was a really nerve-wracking time! The boat of course was swaying a bit in the slight swell, even with it being calm weather. Neither Margaret nor myself like climbing up rope ladders!

On top of all this, Margaret wasn't feeling at all well with her third pregnancy. After we had arrived in Kinngait and landed there, the next day she was told she must overnight in the Nursing Station in Kinngait because of her state, being pregnant about six months. Soon after, she had a miscarriage of a little six-month-old fetus (it was a boy). We were all very concerned about her health.

In the meantime, the carpenter had finished the house and we could all move in with our supplies from Kimmirut and the supplies that had newly arrived – our food for the coming year! For the first time, this included frozen meat, because there was a community freezer in Kinngait. We had known about this before we got to Kinngait, and so could arrange to buy frozen southern meat and have it brought up in the ship's freezer. This would help with our general diet and the food supply. We were made very welcome by the people of Kinngait and we were asked out to many meals, both by Inuit and by non-Inuit. We still had to rely somewhat upon canned fruit and vegetables for ourselves, including those 3-lb cans of very fat bacon!

Our Life in Kinngait

After we had settled in to our rather bare-looking house, it meant spending more time with the Parish. By then I could preach more easily in Inuktitut, and catch up on a backlog of people waiting for marriages and baptisms. Funerals were held from time to time, but there were no suicides in Kinngait. It was more or less unheard-of in those days, although I'm afraid that there were still some cases of suicides, even then. It was a very hard time to have a funeral there, because there was no one designated person to dig graves. My job was to look for volunteers! In winter, it was even harder to dig a grave, as there was no site previously marked out as a graveyard. Instead of that, you had to find a diggable gravel patch. These patches would not freeze up in winter, so it was possible to bury anyone then. The patches were small and they were rather scattered all around the community. The coffins couldn't go very deep into the ground. I am wondering what's happened to all of those coffins scattered around Kinngait. I believe, however, that since we left there, the coffins were re-buried and are now in a permanent graveyard.

There always seemed to be enough local food in Kinngait, and I was often called to a feast being held in a person's house. The feast would often be cutting up raw seal, or digging into walrus meat around the neck and head. It was after a prayer though, to be thankful for the food. I myself in my mind prayed that we would be kept from getting sick from the food. There had been previous cases of trichinosis and even botulism caused by eating infected walrus meat.

At times, when Margaret had prepared a big lunch or something special, I would suddenly be called to a feast. That meant that I had to drop the lunch and go, so that I would not offend the potential host. That must have been hurtful to Margaret, but I really had no choice, as you must not be seen to be looking down upon the hospitality that's given to you. When I was a kid I remember how I used to like to chew on a bit of raw meat and my mother really thought I was weird (she was right!!), but I guess it was some sort of preparation for the future. Sharing in feasts and eating local food and getting to know Inuit culture was a necessary way to be accepted in the community and in the Church. I believe there's not enough today of clergy going to all of the feasts and community events that are held and led by Inuit, because of many "other commitments." Also I know that when I was in Iqaluit, there were so many things to do to keep everything running in the Parish, so when I eventually did get to just make a social visit to a family, they would think that I had come to bring them news of a relative's death!

Then when I was there in Kinngait I started a program to say beforehand that I would be visiting such-and-such a house at such-and-such a time, and hope that I could meet up with all the family then. I would go to a house one week and then to a different house the next week. I would visit, just to talk with the family about their needs as a family, their questions, their concerns, their questions about the Christian Faith and so on. I would then read a few verses from the Bible, have a short prayer and blessing – then leave, encouraging them to continue to keep the Faith. I thought it was important to spend one evening doing this and to be quite honest, I believe that we need to still do this today. Clergy do have to get around to the parishioners and their families!

In 1962 I went all the way back to Kimmirut, not by dog team but by snowmobile. This was when snowmobiles were very new to the North and still could not be fully trusted – so for safety reasons, we also brought a dog team along with us! Besides these winter visits, I went by boat to visit summer fishing and hunting camps. I also went boating with people hunting. I was never a real hunter myself and in my whole life only got one seal and one caribou. I did, however catch birds and rabbits and even a fox. When we went hunting, thinking back about it, it was very dangerous. There are a lot of real treacherous currents going around near Kinngait. I would go hunting by boat with my friend Kooyoo, the one who guided me previously when I was in Kimmirut. We'd go in his canoe and there was no shelter in that canoe at all. I think it was only a 22-footer, and there would be about six or seven men in that one little canoe. At times, because of the currents and a wind going in the opposite direction, the waves would be quite steep. I got a little bit scared of going in that little freighter canoe with all those people. It made the canoe heavily laden in a choppy sea. We always got seals and we always came back safely the next morning! I had to leave Margaret on her own with our kids while I was away hunting.

This is the type of canoe then used for hunting seals (Davidee with his family)

We enjoyed our time in Kinngait, and our two girls started to have real friends there. We had someone who came and helped me with the physical chores. Saggiaq and us were great friends and he really helped us with our daily chores. These were mainly the need of carrying ice from the blocks placed outside our house and putting them into our melting tank inside our house. Then there was the need to keep the "home fires burning" by pumping oil into our 200-gallon fuel oil storage tank from the 45-gallon drums on the beach. This outside tank fed our kitchen and living room stoves. He also dealt with many other maintenance issues.

Margaret's "Adventure"
In 1962, Margaret got pregnant again, soon after her miscarriage. She had to leave the community, because the nurse there wouldn't agree to do the delivery. When it was very apparent Margaret was pregnant, and the nurse wouldn't do the delivery of the babe to be, with no scheduled flights, it meant that

she had to get out somehow. Luckily there was a Coast Guard boat anchored there, our friend the *McLean*! She was able to get on that, but the McLean wasn't going South. Instead, the *McLean*, somehow, was able to meet up with another icebreaker that was going south, the *Montcalm*. Margaret transferred to the *Montcalm* by walking over to it, very pregnant, on a plank in mid-Hudson Strait! She didn't tell me how Sue and Ann got over from the one boat to the other. The Bishop would not hear of me going with Margaret – in those days it was not an option. The name of the *Montcalm* was a misnomer; "calm" – no way! Margaret said that it was the roughest crossing or passage you could imagine, going along the Labrador coast. In fact she had to be strapped in to her bunk with our two little daughters, as it was so rough. When she did finally get to the Montréal docks, another terrible thing happened to her. The baggage that belonged to her somehow got loose whilst being unloaded from the boat to the Dockside, so that it fell right into the St. Lawrence River and got everything wet! An ironical fact was that this happened when it was Thanksgiving Weekend. Its hard to give thanksgiving to the Lord in all circumstances! The stores were closed, so she could not buy replacement clothes.

She got to the hotel, had to hang up her wet money, which had also been in the sunken suitcase, on a line in her room to dry. It looked as if she was making forged notes! She also had to wash and dry all the wet clothes. The next day, after all had dried out in a hotel that she had eventually found, she did get to Toronto by train. What a journey from Kinngait to Scarborough, taking about three weeks.

Margaret then stayed in Scarborough until Pat was born in late November. The birth went ahead as planned, but she didn't get back home until early the next year, 1963. She came back via Moosonee on an Austin Airways DC 3, which in those days seemed a big plane. Austin Airways came right up along the Québec coast, landing at the various communities en route, landing on the sea ice with skis. I think it must've been really strenuous having to make that long flight home, stopping at the various communities all the way up the East Hudson Bay Coast. There was our new baby Pat, together with little Ann and Sue, and going that long cold journey from Moosonee to Kinngait. So it was a joy when she finally got back and we carried on our life together.

Social Change in Kinngait

Our time in Kinngait was a very interesting one. In a way we were in the middle of the change from Stone Age to Space Age. This was the time that Inuit had to leave their traditional small hunting camps to move into the larger communities. Many people were brought in to live in Kinngait so that kids could go to school and parents receive Family Allowance. People moved because the government threatened them that if they didn't send their kids to school, they would be cut off from family and other allowances. In some isolated communities, the government even sent in planes to grab some children and take them away from their family and camps. Dogs were shot so that families would be forced to go and live in a community, as they would be no longer able to do sufficient hunting without their dog teams. I never knew anything about all of this at that time, as we were very cut off from the rest of Canada. It was all very new to me. There was no RCMP detachment in Kinngait until the middle '60s, so we didn't have a problem of killing of dogs by the Police that I know of.

I was happy though, that there were a lot of people there in Kinngait. It meant that I wouldn't have to travel so much to camps – people were already here in Kinngait. I could stay longer at home! Then there were always visitors coming into our house to be served tea, cookies and biscuits. We would catch up on the news and their needs. I found that there were a lot of family problems that needed to be dealt with. When we first arrived, there was no social worker available there. I was so often called to help government officials by translating things between them and the person whom they had gone to see. The government worker did not know Inuktitut. There were health issues, relationship issues and poverty issues, let alone many spiritual issues and questions about our Christian Faith.

It was good that people came and visited us so very much, both Inuit and non Inuit! There were many social issues to work out, especially dealing with marriage and the giving of prospective brides and the taking of wedding ceremonies. At times these meetings were quite tense. It was a new idea that the woman would have a choice as to which man she's going to marry! Looking back, I'm afraid some were more or less cajoled into saying "I do" to their prospective husband. It was the parents' choice for the future husband – not the bride's. Some marriages were still arranged for little kids to get married when they were older. Even our eldest Ann – she doesn't like even thinking of this – was in a semi-serious way supposed to marry a boy called Mosesee. This "arrangement" for the future commitment was made when they were both only two or three years old. We like to joke a little with her to remind her of this "arrangement" made many years ago!

People didn't realize what it all meant. Looking back, I should've given more preparation to those who were getting married and given more teaching to those who weren't!

There was always a clash of original Inuit culture ways and Christian ways regarding marriage and relationships. Women were treated very poorly in so many families, and it was even considered normal for them to be beaten up at times by their husbands. One time, in the morning Margaret and I were just about to get up out of our bed. I think she was up first, and suddenly our front door flew open – we never locked it in those days. It was always open and anyone could come in. One woman, called Mary, rushed in looking terrified and she jumped right into bed with me! It was really sad to know that she was a victim of abuse, and was running away from her husband, who was very mad at her, beating her up for some small reason. She was running away from him and so scared she didn't know what she was doing. Somehow she must have felt that our house was a safe refuge. I'm afraid that many women were beaten up, and many women were scared, even of their own husbands. I have only given you one example of the terror caused by abuse – there were many more similar situations. I cannot accept that the so-called cultural reason for all of this, is just to show the wife as to who is the boss, and to make sure she remains faithful to him – or else!

I spent a lot of time dealing with family counselling – there were no psychologists and government counsellors in those days. Also there were no paid interpreters. You can guess who had to do these things! It was a great opportunity, however, to apply the Gospel message and talk about their need of the Lord in their daily lives.

Then there were many people who were wanting to be helped, and I'd be called out any time, day or night, to homes to try and give that help. Because there were many living together in one community, who had never had that experience before, it all caused many more social problems than when people were more isolated. My friend Simeeonie Koopapik (a Lay Reader in Kinngait) had told me that in the past, when people came in to Kinngait in the summer to wait for the supply boat, whilst waiting, things would get rowdy and problems be created. This was because so many people were suddenly living together in the same community, instead of a few living together in their small isolated camps. When they got back to their camps these problems would vanish. In other words, the government is to blame for the lack of preparation they made to help people settle down into a large community. There were no proper ac-commodation, schooling or health facilities to cater for the sudden influx of people. They had to get used to living in a larger community and the transition was far from easy. I believe that is the reason why we were sent there, to join with others in help-ing the people in these new circumstances. Somehow the Lord wanted us to be there – that's the reason!

We got quite a few drunken episodes. In fact, people used to order booze from Iqaluit and about every 10 days you'd get a chartered Twin Otter plane landing to deliver its cargo of many cases of booze. We were happy when bad weather was there to stop the landing of the plane! It's not hard to imagine the result the next day, after the weather was good and all the booze had been unloaded and delivered to homes. When there wasn't that southern booze, there was some homebrew being made. When people couldn't get homebrew, some of the younger kids, and even older ones, went to sniffing gas. Some even tried to drink methyl hydrate. I knew one person who actually died because he had drunk methyl hydrate.

As there was no RCMP detachment in Kinngait until the mid-'60s, any criminal activity had to be stopped by the people themselves. When an especially serious event had happened, the RCMP plane had to be brought in. The problems that we had mainly boiled down to trying to work out any conflict between the traditional way of living and the new way. Some found it too frustrating so they would take to alcohol, home brew and sniffing gas.

One day I went into a home where there was always a lot of drunkenness, because of the homebrew they were making. No one in there! There was the culprit! A whole 5-gallon wooden barrel, full of homebrew, standing on the floor. I went to it, took it outside and poured it all out onto the ground! I wonder what the occupants of the house thought when they came home and found their homebrew all gone. To this day no one knew of this drastic action that I took – foolish maybe – but tired of getting so many drunks around our house. I would have handled the situation very differently today, because what I did, did not really change things afterwards – only a temporary stop gap measure. That family needed a lot of counselling instead. I must say that it was unusual for me to do something like that, as I am a shy person by nature.

The government representative, Jim Houston, was very kind to the people, and on the whole gave them what they needed or wanted. He had to arrange for some sort of accommodations to be built, because they came in from their camps with just what they could put on to their qamutiit – that was not enough to build a house! Inuit did not usually have many possessions other than rifles, bedding skins and quilts, cooking utensils, qulliit, dog teams, qamutiit and accessories. As far as I remember, the government did supply very basic building kits for some odd-shaped 8 by 12-foot houses to be built – to house families up to about 15 people! There was no plumbing system, power or furniture provided. You will notice a picture of one in Iqaluit, now only used for storage. This one looks immaculate compared with all the run-down ones that used to be in Kinngait. They had a nickname, "Matchbox houses," because so many were pushed into living in them, like matches in a match box! It was very hard for people to adjust to the cramped quarters, also no longer being near to their favourite hunting grounds.

A Matchbox House in Iqaluit – now used for storage (picture courtesy of Susan Gardener)

The reason for coming into communities was so that kids could go to school and parents could receive Family Allowance. As there was no Police detachment to do this in Kinngait, Jim Houston, or his worker, would be assigned to do this. In Kinngait we had a very artistic community, because there were interfamily marriages which produced that result. The real founder of Kinngait was a man called Inukjuakjuk who originally came from Northern Quebec, who had had three wives. Their descendants became the Kingangmiut (Kinngait people). Other people came later.

Schooling in Kinngait

Eventually Government Social Services came to Kinngait. There was only one school building, already there when we first arrived in Kinngait. It just had one teacher (Anne Bernstein – later she became Anne Wyse) and a teacher's aide whose name was Miss Moon. That was for the whole of Kinngait. Only later was a proper school with various classrooms built, which would teach children up to Grade 6. So Margaret and I did not teach a full day school course anymore, but instead of that, there was time to go into the day school and go around the various classes teaching religious education. I got others involved to help, and we spent a whole morning going to the various classes teaching the program. I thought that was a vital part of the ministry to be able to do that. We would include the teaching of syllabics in our curriculum. We could teach the Bible and Christian Faith every day to each class. That was my morning gone!

Simeeonie Koopapik teaching our Christian Faith and syllabics
in Kinngait Day School

As soon as school was out I would grab my parka and go from the school, rush over quite a large hill to where our Mission House was, over to the other side of the hill. Our house was in a place called Quurralaaq, which meant "sometimes a small little brook, other times a big stream." I would try to run non-stop to get exercise. People to this day still remember me trying to run non-stop from the school to our Mission House! When I got home, there was always Margaret ready to greet me after a hard morning of baking bread, finding something to cook for lunch, and looking after our two (later four) children!

Then in addition to going to the Day School, there was Sunday School to deal with. We had to order supplies, to make sure that every person who went to Sunday School would have a take-home paper. We needed materials for over a hundred! Yes, a hundred from cradle to late teenagers. Had to get supplies from the south for each one. I wrote begging letters and Scripture Press responded. They gave us lots of pictures and lesson ideas! I would have Sunday School teachers teaching sessions during the week in our house – three groups. We had primary, inter-mediate and senior groups. I had to arrange the three groups of teachers, who would all come at different times one evening a week for preparation and instruction, for them to be ready to teach Sunday school on the next Sunday. Margaret always came and gave each group tea and cookies. Thankfully by this time there was a plumbing system in our house (except for toilet) and ice blocks had been cut up and put into our holding tank to melt.

I've always found a need for kids to have take-home papers after their lessons. They could talk to their parents about the lessons they were taught. The Sunday School teachers who I taught became increasingly competent, and they gave good lessons in our house and in the Church.

Our Sunday School in our house at Kinngait

In 1964, we had to build an extension on to the Mission House because of all the children and adults coming for the various activities – Sunday School, teachers' preparation classes, ladies' groups, Lay Readers classes, youth work, etc. It also meant that we had to have a warehouse to stack our various supplies, both food for our growing family, as well as a place for Bibles and books and things like that. That was another project for another year –1965–- to build a proper warehouse.

Another challenge was for the choir to be formed and to get ready for the coming Sunday. We had their preparations in our friend Simeonie's house. This was a whole evening once a week. We talked about the coming Sunday and who was doing what. I wanted the services to be shared and lead by various people who had that ability to lead. It must not be just me doing the whole service! Thus I found the necessity of having lay people involved. In those days it was rather the idea of "you are the Minister, so you do it all" – a very colonial idea!

Inuktitut is spoken and understood all over Baffin Island, but there are certain local variations in the words, so the same word can mean different things. I always think of the time in Kinngait when we were at Simeonie's having choir practice, and one of the Lay Readers from Québec was visiting who had a different dialect. He had to leave early whilst we were still practising singing our hymns for the next Sunday. I said in South Baffin Inuktitut "aliasunginavit?" which means, "Are you not scared of ghosts/spirits?" In his dialect he would have thought it meant "Are you going out because you are not happy?" I knew he would be going out on a dark night, by a place that was supposed to be haunted, so I had made my comment in fun. We all burst out laughing! You can see how meanings in various dialects can make for interesting situations!

Catechist School Students

Eventually the Bishop said I had to teach a few lay people in a more formal way, and so in 1966 we had to have a Catechist School built. That was a building about the same size as the Mission House, but it had to accommodate two large families and a little classroom in the middle. So you can imagine, things were a bit crowded! It amazes me, looking back, how those who stayed there were always thankful to be there, in spite of the poor living conditions with very basic food provided by the Diocese. I had three very willing students: Eeyetseak and his father Kooyoo, and Akishook (from Iqaluit). Another time I was given two people from Québec to teach. Eventually the one from Povungnirtuq was ordained, so it was a blessing that we could have this Catechist School.

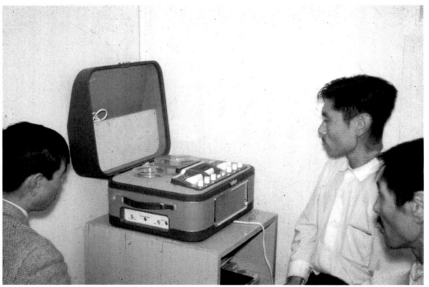

First Catechist School Students –L-R Akeeshook, Eeyeetseak and Kooyoo

This need to train Lay Readers more, on top of all of the other things I had to do, and also to look after my family all made quite a heavy load on my plate. But still more to come! The Bishop wanted me to travel around the North with him, as sort of companion or aide, to take a lot of the services. One of my most embarrassing moments with him was in Arctic Bay. I was helping the Bishop at a Communion service and something terrible happened. He had been gloating about how he liked to use ordinary juice bottles for the Communion wine and water (rather than having to buy the expensive, traditional silver-plated ones). The juice bottles he used had the tops that screwed on to the base of the jar one third of the way down. Serving the Bishop at Communion, I held onto the top third, apparently attached to the bottom two-thirds of the bottle. "Apparently" is the word! As I handed the wine to him, the so-called attached top came right off before he could grab the bottom part. In front of everybody, the bottom part went crashing down to the Sanctuary floor, spilling most of the wine. I wonder if that stain on the floor is still there to this day!

The Bishop also wasn't a well person. He had colitis and had to have a green bag as a result of his colitis. Every community we went to, no person got out first, it was the green bag with its contents that was thrown out first! In spite of his colitis, he had the heart to do the very best for the people, and he did a good job at that. We had a pilot called Roley who could be a little tight, shall we say – not drunken, but a bit woozy, and he had to often navigate by the direction of the sun. We were going over great high mountains peaks, zooming far down to icy fiords below. You could see way, way down to the ground, when we were going along the north Baffin coast. That was scary, in an insignificant small plane waving about in the wind above this field of pointed, rugged, wind-swept peaks of the mountainous country below. I was very thankful when we got away from that type of terrain to the more friendly look of Kinngait – and home!

Margaret Keeps the "Home Fires" Burning

This travelling around with the Bishop was not good for the Parish of Kinngait, but I couldn't argue with Bishop Marsh – he was the boss! Whilst I was away, Margaret had to keep the "home fires" burning, looking after our house and our children. Then she had many other things to do, whether I was there or not. She had to do all her baking and cooking to feed our family; no bread at the store. She also ran the Women's Association – WA it was called then, ACW (Anglican Church Women) now. She had to lead this group and take a devotion every week until, later on, the ladies themselves could do it. Whilst I was away she still taught Sunday School in English and prepared the three groups of teachers for their classes. Then she had to deal with the clothing, quilts and many other items, which were sent up to our Mission in big bales, by some hard working WA ladies in the South. All of these items were a true blessing for many, who had so little of their own possessions. Because people from camps had to live in Kinngait, away from good hunting grounds, the hunters didn't hunt so much. It meant families became poorer. You can see how happy the ladies in the following picture are with some items they were given from the bales! The ladies at the Church we go to in Ottawa are still collecting clothes, bedding, toiletries etc. for bales for the North. This is because the need is still there. People hooked on alcohol and drugs, as well as being unemployed, often spend too much money on their habits. The family suffers, especially the children. They do still need this extra help!

Ladies (in Kimmirut) who had just been given items from the ACW Bales

Now we had three children and all the Parish work. That was quite stressful and I don't think the Bishop realized that. Added to all of this, the Bishop had wanted me to start up this Catechist School for Lay Readers, which would take up a lot of my time teaching the three students he sent there for training. There was still the Parish work with services, teaching, counselling etc., plus my "tours" with him, plus time to be with my family. But the Lord gave us strength and let us carry on without having to go south because of exhaustion. That's the way it was then!

Second Holiday Adventures

We eventually went on a holiday in 1966. At the start of this holiday, we suffered the most scary time that you could imagine. We were all going by boat to England. Whilst coming from the North and waiting to board the boat, we stayed with the Tincomes and enjoyed their wonderful hospitality. They helped us to get to the place where a special bus for people going overseas would leave for the docks, and our credentials checked. When we got to this large "waiting place" for documents etc., there were crowds of people also waiting for this special bus for the docks. Margaret was not feeling well and between us we had Ann, Sue and Pat. Whilst we were waiting to be called by Immigration, Margaret was more or less laying down and feeling very yucky with some flu bug – then – all of a sudden – no Pat! She was only three years old. I did not notice that she had disappeared – black mark, Dad! She'd wandered off, and of course in this crowd, where could she have gone? I was very scared and didn't know what to do. Our turn for Immigration could be called at any moment, but whatever happened we could not leave without Pat. But by the grace of the Lord (and to this day I don't know how else to explain what happened next) a policeman came to us with Pat to bring her back to us! I cannot humanly explain how he could find her and bring her back to us, she being just a tiny blob amongst the great crowd of people waiting there!

We were cleared with Customs and got on the boat, the *Empress of Britain*. Margaret could finally lie down and see the ship's doctor and start our voyage to England. She got better after a few days on the boat, and we enjoyed the passage without any further problems. One memory always stands out to me from that voyage: there is our daughter Pat, at three years old, solo dancing to entertain three or four hundred people in the lounge of the *Empress*, to the music of "The Yellow Submarine" – priceless! She was not shy! We then had a three-month holiday in England from the middle of June to mid-September, and then we would go back to Kinngait.

In the meantime, whilst we were in England, we stayed in a rented house, which my Aunt Ada had arranged for us in Hythe, Kent. Also whilst there we were able to bring my mother from a nursing home in Sunbury-on-Thames (it was near Egham) run by the government. She wasn't in Woolston any longer, because my father had died in 1961. This meant that my mother had to be put into a home. It wasn't a very nice one in Sunbury-on-Thames. We went and fetched her so she could transfer to a much nicer nursing home in Hythe. I remember the cost. It was 25 guineas – (25 pounds and 25 shillings). I have forgotten whether this amount was per week or per month!

We also had a time in Newquay enjoying the wonderful beaches and surfing. We also went to stay with Margaret's parents in Frith Common, and let our three children go cherry picking from the many trees in "Grandpa's orchard." We had a good holiday because I didn't have to do any deputation work! People were very interested about the Arctic and many still thought that Inuit lived in snow houses all through summer and winter.

Back to Kinngait: Margaret's Circular Letter

Then we had to get back to Kinngait. I had to get back to deal with the waiting Catechist School students, let alone all the Parish work waiting for me. The following extract from a General Circular letter that Margaret wrote in the Fall of 1968 tells us about the typical life of a young guy in Kinngait in 1968 through his eyes:

I have just finished unloading the last barge from the supply boat. We have been working day and night for four days, except at low tide. At low tide the barge cannot unload – so we can sleep then. With 15 others I have been carrying all the many cartons of food, cigarettes, candy, washing machines, skidoos and canoes from the beach to the warehouse. We have had several ships here during the summer, bringing in all that the settlement needs. For the past few years, many new houses have come, and I wonder if any more will come this year. I have already moved into a three-bedroom house. I was born, 30 years ago, in an igloo. I never dreamt that one day I would be living in such a large house with electricity and oil burning stove. Recently Bell telephone came and fixed a phone in my house. The next thing I would like to have is one of those little refrigerators that some of my friends got last year.

Yesterday as I unloaded the supplies, I could not but help think of all the changes that have taken place in the past 20 years. Yesterday two planes came here, one from Frobisher and one from Moosonee, which brings in the mail once a month. This one landed on the water, but the one from Frobisher landed on the airstrip that was made this summer. Its only a "dirt strip", and we all wondered if the plane could land and then take off again. However, all was well, and so now for the first time, we need not be isolated, even at break-up or freeze-up time.

You may wonder what I do for a living. No, I do not hunt or trap very much any more. I work in the settlement, drive a tractor, or do whatever work I can. Sometimes I make the stone carvings that the white people like to buy. Sometimes I go out and get the stone to carve with, or sometimes I buy it from the store at 10 cents per pound. Some of my friends work at the Co-op and carve soapstone printing blocks from which the famous Cape Dorset prints are made. Print fabric samples are also made here with Eskimo designs. My wife and other women make drawings for the prints. Many more Eskimos now are getting permanent jobs. There are very few of my friends who are just depending on hunting for a living. Some people work permanently for the stores or for the Government agencies. I go hunting when I can and it is good to get away from the settlement for a while in a canoe. I have an outboard motor and so can get away when I want to. Gasoline is very expensive here, 95 cents a gallon, so hunting trips can be expensive. In the springtime I take my family down the coast for a month when the fishing is good. In the winter I have a skidoo, and sometimes go hunting with this. Some of my friends have got Hondas™ this past year. This is something new for us, and I would like to have one this next year. I shall have to do lots of carving!

I devote some time to Church work. Sunday is a busy day with Church services, and then I help teach one Sunday School group. I also sing in the choir with about 18 others. We have choir practice once a week at one of my friend's homes. In summer some still go away to the old summer camps, and so there are not so many in church as in the winter months. Last year we had to extend our Church because during the winter it was so full. We thought that we would like to do this completely on our own, and so bought the necessary materials at the local store. Then during the best weeks of summer my friends and I did the building. Some gave up a day or two of work, and others did it in their free time. We were very happy to be able to have completed the whole project ourselves.

During the week I find lots to do when not hunting or working. On Monday evenings I go to the Minister's house to get help with the next week's Sunday School lesson. Three others and myself are the last of the 18 teachers to go. We arrive about 10 PM, and it is not often that we leave before midnight.

On Tuesday I go to the [Church] Youth group. I go to help the Minister and some other older men to help at the meetings. Sometimes we have English and Eskimo games, other times talks about the Bible, or discussions and readings about God's action in the world today. I really enjoyed listening to our Minister when he read in Eskimo the book The Cross and the Switchblade to us. We also practice hymns and choruses with a guitar group. We have a special youth service once a month with the guitar group playing for the hymns. On Wednesdays I sometime go to the adult religious education classes that the Minister holds – I am afraid I don't go as often as I should. The minister tells us about Church history and other things of interest about our belief. Sometimes it is our turn to have the mid-week prayer meeting in our house. We always know when it is our turn and so we can ask others to join us. The way I am going on you would think that I am always doing Church work – this is not so. We have movies in the Community Hall three times a week and I like to go. There is the Go-Go Club, and this is open every day of the week, except Sunday. I go there to play pool. Sometimes I play cards and stay up too late and gamble too much. The plane sometimes brings beer and liquor and some of us drink too much and then do things of which afterwards we are ashamed. It is a comfort to know that we can always turn to Christ as Saviour for forgiveness at such times. We would ask that you would pray that our faith would be strengthened at times of temptation to turn more to Christ as Lord as well. I must stop now - I saw that the boat had brought in some cartons of fresh fruit and maybe the store Manager will be selling them soon. I wouldn't want to miss this once-a-year treat!

Margaret then notes in her letter:

As you see there is always a conflict of various pressures for his leisure time. The amount of conflict varies with age. The young teenager has little to do and is often bored with life in a settlement. One young man even told us he would like to go to prison in the South, because of the gymnasium and other recreational facilities there. It is our task to make the challenge of Christ go into all their time. For those in full employment, leisure time is more taken up with things that are natural to them – hunting and fishing. Some are very conscious of their responsibility to give some of their leisure time to Church work, but others find it difficult when there are so many counter-attractions for their leisure time. We are still spending our time in training leaders for Church work in the Parish. The latest stage in this work is in our training those who will undertake Parish visiting.

Then Margaret goes on to talk a little about our family – interesting that she talks about our eldest daughter's need to get help with her English as her first language is Inuktitut!

In 1969, Social Services had a four-year-old boy, named Kym, who they didn't know what to do with. They had put him, after his mother had died at childbirth, into the "care" of a very deaf elderly lady called Anna. Kym's father and the others weren't looking after Kym properly. Anna could not communicate with Kym very well, and she had no one to provide her and Kym with country food. So Kym was not fed properly there either. Social Services wanted him to be placed with us just for a few months' trial, so that he could learn Inuktitut and English with our family. Inuktitut was our girls' first language! So he was with us for that last year we had in Kinngait. He adapted very well to our family, and we to him.

In 1970, the time came for us to have to move from Kinngait. The Bishop had arranged for us to go to Pangnirtung, and there was a special reason for this. It was so that I could be in charge of a theological training college called the Arthur Turner Training School (ATTS). So once again Margaret, the four children and myself had to pack up. We were very sorry to leave Kinngait. We loved being there, a most interesting place with very interesting artistic people. The Lord blessed the work and many people were converted to truly follow the Lord. We felt very much at home and part of the community. There had never been a resident Minister living there. We were so thankful that we were called to be the first ones there, and felt that we could leave it in good hands with the lay people after we had left.

In those days there was no alternative Church there, although very soon after we left there was one, a Glad Tidings Church. Also just before we first arrived in Kinngait in 1960, the Roman Catholic Mission and their priest left. I'd never had experience of more than one Church in a community. That spoiled me. I didn't really understand all the issues.

CHAPTER 4: PANGNIRTUNG AND THE ARTHUR TURNER TRAINING SCHOOL

Our Move To Pangnirtung and the ATTS

A view of Pang. Photo credit: David Kilabuk Photography

It was in the summer of 1970 that a plane was chartered for us: first to Iqaluit, where we stayed overnight, and then to go on to Pangnirtung. We flew in a plane like a boxcar. It was called a SkyVan. We got to Pangnirtung without any incident and landed on a very short runway – part of it was being dug up! I remember the beautiful sunny evening when we did arrive there at the beginning of July. There was a crowd of people to greet us and this made us feel at home. Then we were taken to the Mission House, all six of us. We settled down there, but I could not take too long doing this, because I was expected to teach at the Arthur Turner Training School (ATTS) as soon as possible. I often think that when the Bishop asked me to be the Principal of ATTS, how I was the most unlikely person for that position. I thought that was quite amusing. God must have been smiling, because when I did my General Ordination Exam in England, just before ordination, I barely scraped through and got only 40% in Doctrine. So the Bishop took a real risk on me! I felt, "Why me — Principal?" I had to rely a lot on the students, as it was so often the students teaching the Principal things!

At this time of writing, only two of the original six students are still alive. Only one of these six students was bilingual. There was no curriculum set out and we were put in a sectioned-off part of the old Church for our classes and worship. We had two or three tables, eight chairs and a chalkboard. That's about all there was. I found that it was a very interesting group of ordinands. Bible study was the main thing we did, and I'm glad, as it laid a great foundation for their future ministry. Then the students also had to be involved in practical work. They would go to various houses, using my weekly visitation schedule, so that all houses in the Parish were eventually visited. They would talk about and teach the need for Jesus in our daily lives as families and individuals. The students would then come back and we'd discuss the various situations, pray about them and help each other to know what's best to do. I'd involved the students as much as possible in all our life together. They would take services every day in ATTS. Very soon they also partook in Church services on a Sunday, choir practice, Sunday school work and any community events. I wanted them to be very visible in the community, and at the same time they'd get hands-on training. I believe that was what was most necessary. I feel today the theological colleges are too academic, and maybe get too involved in studies not relevant to everyday living. There needs to be more emphasis on the whole meaning of being ordained as a Shepherd of the Flock. There is always the need for the Gospel to be really lived out and preached!

The first graduated Ordinands – Ipeelie Naparktuk, Eliyah Keenainak, Jimmy Muckpah, Tommy Suluk (not ordained), Timothy Kalai

One of the students was not very responsive and he had to eventually drop out, so I was left with five. Tommy, one of the five, was not old enough for ordination, although he completed the whole course of two years.

In Pangnirtung it was not easy, because I had to be with the students most of the time. When I first got there, I obviously was expected to help organize many events and activities in the Parish. Most of the things we had done in Kinngait we tried to do in Pangnirtung. The Bishop said I should be very well off because I had six Curates to help me! In practice it didn't work out like that.

Bishop Marsh made his annual visit one year, which would have been his last visit before he died in 1972. There was something that he didn't like about what I'd done or had not done, while I knew that I had done my best. So I said to him, "Bishop Marsh, I feel that I should quit, but I won't, because I serve a higher authority than you." And that was a punch below the belt for him, and he answered, "Mike, that's a good answer," and we were all right after that!

I also wanted to give proper attention to my family! Here were my three daughters and Kym growing up, almost without a father. More work for Margaret. Did the Bishop really understand? No! I had the Parish work to do as well, plus the training of the students, so the day became very short to fit in everything. At times, some parishioners who wanted to see me had to be told to come back at 10 o'clock that night. Then there was always the need to deal with correspondence and financial matters of the Parish. The Parish was struggling to be self-supporting. That was a challenge. Then there was the Bishop, who was still being difficult. Bishop Marsh did odd things, like wanting to put an oil tank on top of the roof of the ATTS building. ATTS by this time had moved into the vacated spaces of the old St. Luke's Hospital, which had to close down in early 1972. Of course that oil tank on top of the roof of the training school didn't last all that long. It had to be brought down!

There was always a need to have suitable materials to train the students. There was nothing much to study with, other than the Bible, a prayer book and hymn book written in Inuktitut syllabics. Most of the first group of students were monolingual. There was one exception to this – Thomas Suluk. He was very fluent and fully bilingual, so he was a real blessing to have there, and he helped the students and myself a lot.

Our First Long-Distance Phone Call

Continuing about the Bishop – it's funny we keep on mentioning him. I hope he's not turning in his grave! Until early 1972, we didn't have any direct communication with the outside world. That's when the Anik satellite was launched and we got a phone that we could use for reaching beyond just the community we were in. In the early spring of 1972, we were, for the first time, able to phone long distance. I mention this because there's a story now that I want to tell. In 1972 the Bishop was in England and his car had struck some mangel-wurzels which had fallen off onto the road from a farmer's truck, lying on a country road. I believe the driver of the Bishop's car tried to swerve to avoid them, and somehow this made the car's door open, and the Bishop fell out. He was sent to St. Luke's Hospital for Clergy in London. We did hear he was there after his accident. Margaret and I thought, when we got long distance for the first time, "Who can we phone to celebrate?" And then we thought, "Ah! We know! We will go and phone St. Luke's Hospital in London to find out how the Bishop is and wish him well." So that's what we did, but when the phone was answered by someone in that hospital, they told us he died just one hour before!

Well, that was news to us. It also turned out that it was also news to everybody else in Canada! No one had known this, so we phoned the Arctic office in Toronto to say, "Hey! We just heard Bishop Marsh has died, assume you know." No! They hadn't known at all. So we thought that was the end of it. But, then we got nasty letters from the Bishop's wife, saying that we had no right to tell the people in the Arctic office about the death of

Bishop Marsh. It should've been announced by the British Embassy first. Our first long distance phone call really backfired on us!

Bishop Marsh had it in his heart to help the Inuit and the Church in the North, to preach the Gospel to many. This was in spite of his sickness and colitis. He only just managed to get around from one place to another by plane and boat. It was very stressful for him, being a person who was not well, but the Lord used him very much in spite of the problems. He truly loved the Lord, the Arctic and its people.

He was finally replaced in 1974 by Bishop Sperry, who we had met before, whilst we were going out on furlough in 1960. This was before he was Bishop, when he was returning to Kugluktuk. He and I became great friends, and he wanted me to go around with him on his travels. This was because he was a Western Arctic Inuktitut-speaking person, and the dialect is quite different from that of the Eastern Arctic. It meant that I had to help him. That was on top of my other activities whilst we were in Pangnirtung.

People in Pangnirtung thought we were very rich, and so they didn't want to pay for utilities and things for our Mission House. It was the policy of the Diocese that self-supporting Parishes had to pay the Minister's salary and government employers' contributions, as well as maintaining the Mission House, the Church, and paying for all utilities on top of all of this. This was all a very hard sell, and they thought that I was gouging them, even when my salary was one of the lowest that an Anglican Minister could have!

There was a very nice Church built there when the Rev. John Marlow was the Minister in the '60s. Whilst we were in Pangnirtung, it used to be full to overflowing for most services (200-300 people) with a beautiful choir of about 30 (men, women and girls). The singing was wonderfully uplifting and enthusiastic. There were some very fine Christian ladies and men there, who really helped lead the worship service. This was indeed the result of a legacy from past missionaries, like the Turner brothers, who had spent many years in the Arctic preaching and teaching people. I'll never forget the beautiful, blended voices of those people singing there. You just can't beat it! It was a wonderful place for the students to train. The first group of students was ordained in 1972. After they had graduated and were ordained, and the Parish seemed to be on a steady course, with lay people leading services and some trained to do counselling, that meant we could go on furlough to England. This was after having been six years without a holiday!

We went on the *Queen Elizabeth 2*, simply referred to as the QE2! There were all six of us. We had a wonderful time on that boat and our kids loved the experience. Our daughters liked plain food – it was not plain food on the QE2. The waiters could not believe it when our daughters only wanted to order spaghetti with nothing added to it whatsoever!

Then we went to London, England, where we also had a great time, then on to Margaret's parents, before going to Newquay in Cornwall. Kym went with us. It was fascinating, getting him seeing things for the first time in the south. Kym had a chest and sinus condition, which gave him a runny nose nearly all the time. But after having fun swimming and playing games on the sands of Newquay, it all completely cleared up!

The Second Group of ATTS Students

We came back to Pangnirtung to start another training school group, another group of ordinands: four this time. One of the four was someone who went to Iqaluit to eventually become the Dean of the Cathedral, Jonas Alooloo. The second one became the Bishop of the Arctic, The Right Reverend Andrew Ataagutaaluk. The third one was an assistant Bishop, Benjamin Arreak. The fourth one finished his course, but did not actually get ordained, which was a real shame. Maybe he, Simon, will be ordained in the future. Andrew, Jonas and Benjamin all worked very well together with the Canadian Bible Society so that the CBS could produce a completely new Bible in Inuktitut. This all took many years of working on this project, and I do feel that their student days at ATTS helped them for this future work.

Our second group of ordinands – Jonas, Andrew, Ben and Simon

Our second group of students was a very responsive group, and I enjoyed the time teaching them. They also taught me a lot! We had some very deep debates over Biblical words and their equivalent meaning in Inuktitut. We also studied and talked about Church history and about running a parish, and things like that. It was very interesting to compare Church history in general with the story of the Church in the Arctic. It was especially useful to look at pre-Christian religion in the North and compare it with our Christian Faith today. There is such a tendency to blame Christian workers for "spoiling" the "religion" and culture that was in the North before Christian missionaries came there. This topic produced some good discussion and learning!

Indeed, we who are Christian make Christ and His Way the only true way, but we do not despise ancient culture, as long as it is in the same spirit of Christianity, and does not take the place of our Christianity. Many customs that went on before Christianity arrived might have been materially good for those lucky enough to be well equipped and independent. However, there were many others, especially women and orphans, who did not have that luxury; they were treated badly and made to be very much a servant of the "rich." Many also lived in fear of evil spirits and fear of the angakkuit (shamans) and fear of breaking taboos. I really believe those who blame missionaries for bringing the Gospel to the North have looked at the past with rose-tinted spectacles!

Pangnirtung Joys and Problems

We had fun in Pangnirtung in spite of all we had to do and some people who were hard to deal with. Our children became teenagers growing up there. We had to look after them, or maybe, they were looking after us! Margaret was really, really busy looking after GA (Girls' Auxiliary) and JA (Junior Auxiliary), Sunday School, cooking and cleaning and everything you can imagine. When Bishop Sperry saw us in that old Mission House, he thought that was the end of that Mission House – we needed to have a new one! So he sent in a carpenter and helper to build the new Mission House. The result was a two-storey palatial new Mission House, constructed for us to enjoy after living in the old one. I think it was in 1975 that happened. So that meant that our family could have more of their own space. It meant a more luxurious heating system and we were all much better in spirits.

Our wonderful new Mission House in Pangnirtung

In the Fall of 1976, Margaret developed a serious problem with possible cancer of the uterus. This meant that she had to be medevacked to Montréal. It was a very hard decision not to go with her. Our children at home needed a parent, and we couldn't take them all out together on the plane. Later Montréal Hospital confirmed that she did indeed have a progressive cancer in the uterus, but it was completely removed by her having a total hysterectomy. She returned to Pangnirtung and carried on again with all the work she was doing before the operation, bless her.

In the Spring of 1976, we went on another holiday. It seems that we were going on holidays all the time! However it was necessary to get away and get refreshed. There was nothing especially sensational about that holiday in '76.

We returned to do the work, but by then Bishop Sperry was truly sympathetic to what was going on with us, doing all these things that were humanly impossible to do properly. I had to trust very much for strength and guidance from the Lord and

Him alone! Bishop Sperry, to solve this problem, provided another person to take the Principalship of the Arthur Turner Training School. Another group of students came there in 1976. The new Principal was Harold Seigmiller along with his wife, Betty. They were a great couple. Later on, when there were problems with Harold's health, he had to leave. He was replaced by Peter Bishop, who taught another group of students. Then last of all was Roy Bowket, who taught a final group of students.

Since then, ATTS has moved to Iqaluit. I am thankful that there have been other Inuit who have now been trained there for ordination. This training is now recognised as part of Nunavut Arctic College's official courses. There was a full time Principal giving it his full-time attention, with five students, who have now graduated and been ordained. At the time of writing this, the ATTS Principal Joey Royal has been made a Bishop, so I am not sure about the immediate future of ATTS in Iqaluit. I am thankful that the set-up for ATTS is very different from my pioneering days with ATTS – even having got Government of Nunavut recognition to cover most costs! It's part of an answer to my original prayer, which I used to say to people, let alone to God, "My aim is to work myself out of a job!" By that I meant that Inuit would be trained and in charge of Parish life in the North. This would be not just for Inuktitut services, but for many Parish activities directed to Inuit and non-Inuit alike. We have to recognize, more and more each year, the number of non-Inuit who do come North, and make the Arctic their home and the Arctic Churches their home also. So we have to really think of them and have clergy trained, ready for them, as well as for those already truly living in the North.

Looking back at our time in Pangnirtung, it was hard in some ways. All was going well at ATTS and generally in the Parish. Because things were going well, you expect opposition from those who don't like to see the Christian Faith upheld so much. I was a good target for opposition. Besides all my many shortcomings, there was one thing I was unjustly accused of, and that was murder! One family there started a rumour after their father had died, saying that I had murdered their father. That false accusation was really in the way of the spread of the Gospel. It was one sign of Jesus' words when He said that His followers must expect false accusations and even to be hated (see Matthew 5:11). Being falsely accused in a way confirmed that we were there for the sake of the Gospel. To this day I don't know how and exactly as to why they dreamed up this false accusation. I can only think that it was from when we travelled to camps; it was common then, for people who visited camps, to take a First Aid kit, and this would include some Aspirin™ or Tylenol™, to give out to people with headaches or the flu. I must have given these Aspirin or Tylenol to the gentleman, who later died because of the flu or pneumonia. This made me a convenient scapegoat! No one died as a result of my having given them Tylenol or Aspirin! Bishop Sperry helped me and gave me all the support possible to clear my name. We were enabled by the Lord to do all that was needed to be done and we give thanks to this day.

I believe a lot of our family have their real background from Pangnirtung. This is both good and bad. At school, our daughters had a very hard time. A lot of the kids there were very "wild," beating-up others at recess and after school. Our daughters had to really be protected, as well as protecting themselves. What made it all worse was the fact that the Principal himself had hangovers, and most of the teachers did not want to be bothered with non-Inuit kids. They said that they came just for the Inuit. Some of the teachers at that time spent most of the day showing movies and let the kids play games. Even more than this, we had to fight to get our children taught Grade 7; the school curriculum in the North, in those days, believe it or not, stopped at Grade 6. Our daughters, when they reached Grade 7, had to follow a compromise "solution," by being alone learning from various text books, with very little guidance. They were "outsiders" in the school. Not good for a young teenager.

As this situation was not satisfactory, the Bishop arranged through the Anglican Church for Ann and Sue to be boarded with a couple near Crystal Beach in Ontario. However this did not work out well, and so for the following year Margaret and I arranged with a couple who happened to be visiting Pangnirtung that they would let Ann and Sue board with them. Then they would continue schooling in their local school in London, Ontario. You can imagine how terribly homesick our daughters were! In the first year it must have been terribly hard for them around Christmas time, when they could not go home. However, for the second year, Archbishop Scott arranged for their fares to be paid, so that they could be home for Christmas. Archbishop Scott was the Primate for the whole Anglican Church in Canada. It shows what a wonderful person he was; even in this position he cared for and helped one little family in the Arctic. This trip home for Christmas was a real blessing. It was quite a culture shock for our two daughters to go from the more informal ways of the North to the stricter rules of the South. However, Sue stuck it out to graduate there with Grade 13, although Ann went instead to be a boarding student in Iqaluit, even when we were still living in Pangnirtung.

Pangnirtung is the place that our daughters remember most of all. They don't really remember so much of Kinngait as Pangnirtung. This is especially true of Pat, who married Archie Angnakak at a very special service two days before Christmas in 1980 – he came from Pangnirtung. That meant that there were a lot of family connections, as he came from a very large family, both by adoption and by birth. People in Kinngait, though, do fondly remember our daughters as they often played together as children.

After some further time in Pangnirtung, Bishop Sperry said that, because ATTS had sort of run out of suitable candidates for ordination, he thought that it would be good if we moved to a place that needed us more. That place was Iqaluit. I know now that it was very hard for our children to move from Pangnirtung, with all their friends there, and as teenagers it was extra hard. Margaret did not want to move, and she said that you can still see the footprints from her, as she was being dragged all over the hills from Pangnirtung to Iqaluit! She didn't want to go to Iqaluit. In the past, when people were going to a community other than Iqaluit, and had to pass through Iqaluit, they would all say, "Let's get out of Iqaluit as quickly as we can. We don't want to stay there!" It had a very bad name originally. That's not so true now, but then it was rather talked about, so that's why she dragged her heels all the way. However, she settled down very well living there. As I write this in Ottawa, she still often says "I want to go home" – meaning Iqaluit!

CHAPTER 5: OUR IQALUIT LIFE

About The Original St Jude's Cathedral

We all moved to Iqaluit in July, 1981, on a DC-3 plane co-chartered with the HBC. We arrived to a Mission House that the Rev. Don Whitbread had built in the '70s. It was a bit run-down with only a "honey bucket" for a toilet. Different from our new house in Pangnirtung! The bucket had a green garbage bag inside it. Every day there would be a "Honey Bag Collector" coming into our house and bathroom to collect the bag. He tramped through the hallway into the bathroom, and as he left you prayed that the bag would not burst (that did happen to some unlucky people)! You also prayed that when you had to use the honey bucket that there would not be a bitterly cold wind blowing down the vent pipe! The honey bucket regime only lasted a few years until a kind parishioner there installed a proper flush toilet and pump-out system.

St Jude's Cathedral had opened for services in 1972, but was constructed in 1971. I heard that there were a lot of problems with getting the supplies unloaded, because of ice on the sealift unloading/loading beach. This made unloading supplies there virtually impossible. Instead supplies had to be off-loaded in nearby Apex, this being the only place where there was a little open water. I have also been told that the whole upper structure, called the Lantern, was suspended in the air by a helicopter and lowered down onto the top of the circular walls that had just been constructed. The Lantern was a large circular Plexiglas structure to give daylight into the interior of the Cathedral. There were no other windows. I can imagine the relief when it was finally in place and fitted on to the circular walls of the Cathedral that had already been constructed and were waiting for the Lantern to be placed on top of them.

One Inuk man was appointed to oversee all the workers and volunteers. He was Markoosee Peter. The incumbent, the Rev. Canon Don Whitbread, along with Markoosee and his builders, did sensational and unique work, later to be used and enjoyed by many local people and visitors. These visitors would include the Royal Family, Prime Ministers, Archbishops, etc., from all around the world. But it was most of all the local people who loved and enjoyed our Cathedral.

The original St. Judes Cathedral

Interior of St. Jude's Cathedral with our choir

Synod meeting in the Cathedral (showing the
bearded Rev Canon Don Whitbread)

In the picture above from the Synod meeting, you get a glimpse of some of the beautiful hangings in the Sanctuary of the Cathedral. Each of the six panels was made by a Parish's ACW group (Anglican Church Women) to illustrate Northern Church life. There were six different Parishes from all over the Diocese of the Arctic who were commissioned to create a panel. It was a very tense moment, it was said, when one panel had not arrived before the official opening of the Cathedral in 1972. A temporary one was hastily sewn and no one knew the difference! The Queen even attended that service. I did not meet her then as I had to be in Pangnirtung with the ATTS students, but I did meet her when she came back later to Iqaluit to celebrate the creation of Nunavut. She is a very observant lady. She noted that our narwhal cross was missing a little piece of the tusk at the top. She said that her tusk in Buckingham Palace was better than ours because it was in perfect condition. I had never noticed the chipped cross myself, yet I had looked at that cross hundreds of times.

On the outskirts of Iqaluit, the community of Apex was the original place where the HBC and Government built in the area. It was quite a long way from the DEW Line Site located at (then) Frobisher Bay, and about three miles away from our Mission House. There was a nice little Church there, St. Simon's, built in 1958. Our Parish was therefore called St. Simon's and St. Jude's. So there we were, arriving from Pangnirtung, to quite a different situation. I wanted to really deal with it and tackle it. On the other hand, I was feeling so very inadequate. I had no car to get around. There were roads and some people did have cars or trucks. Instead of a car, I had a three-wheeler motorbike. Today that would be banned, but at that time they were legal. When it was very cold I'd use a snowmobile, especially when I had to go to Apex Church to take a service. I would go there every Sunday at night. When I was getting from Iqaluit to Apex, I had to go down the big Apex hill and I'd go on my little three-wheeler. In those days it was a gravel road, so I'd speed around a bend and the cloud of dust that was piling up behind me as I sped, would be like a signal to say "I'm nearly there – get the service started!"

Parish Activities in Iqaluit

There were many activities going on Sundays. This meant that I could only finally make it to Apex right on 7 o'clock or a little after. I was never early because I had so much to do on a Sunday. The morning service in the Cathedral would be at 10 o'clock and it would be in the English language. The very first service I did in English there brought only about eight people. It would be a short one, about 30 minutes. Then the second one in Inuktitut would start at 11 o'clock, and that might be two hours long. After that and clearing up and everything, got home for lunch at 1:15, with family and some friends of our family. Margaret had got all that ready. Sometimes they couldn't really wait for me because they were so hungry and I was so slow.

Then I had to eat my lunch quickly and be at the hospital by 2 o'clock, where I'd go around to the people who were in bed to find out those who could get out of bed. They would go then to a ward in which were the people who couldn't get out of bed. We'd have a service in that ward, wherever that happened to be. We were rather crammed into that space! I did make almost daily hospital visits during the week, so I knew most of the patients and staff from those visits. This also helped us to be more ready for Sunday. In those days it was still the old 1962-built Baffin Regional Hospital and there was no Chapel. Even today, in the beautiful new hospital, there is still no Chapel as such.

After that service of about 35 minutes, I had arranged to go to the Baffin Correctional Centre (BCC) for a service at 3 p.m. There, I could talk to a very good, captive congregation! I didn't do much visiting with the inmates on a Sunday, because I made a point of making my rounds at BCC each Saturday in the afternoon. I would go to the various rooms they had, which held six or eight people. I found that they were very receptive listeners to the Gospel message, also open for being counselled and prayed for. That's where the real work was, to let them know that, whatever they'd done in the past, they were truly forgiven sinners, because of the Lord Jesus dying for each one of them. Quite a few inmates committed their lives to Him. I always had a helper with me to help with the singing, mainly Annie Tiglik, who was always very faithful in coming to help me. Usually we sang without accompaniment, but sometimes did get a guitarist to play.

After the time at BCC I would have to go to Ukkivik for 4 p.m. This was the residence where students from other communities came and had to stay while they attended high school in Iqaluit, because there was no equivalent study available in their own home community. After these commitments I would go home for supper and then try and get to Apex Church on time. Sometimes I even had to go after Apex Church service to the women's shelter, Qimaavik, where women went when they were in a violent relationship with a husband or boyfriend. I counselled them and prayed for them. So much more I could have done. I felt very inadequate. There were so many other people who wanted to talk, to be prayed for and to understand our faith better.

Some people used to think, "Boy! Mike's got it easy! Only works one day a week." Ha! Ha! In some ways Sunday was my easy day, because during the week I had to do preparation work, spend some time at home in the morning , working out lessons for children, for Lay Readers, for translation work and for home Bible study groups. Monday evening was the ladies' night, the ACW, which I didn't really partake in, except once a month I'd go and give a short talk there. In about 1983 Methusalah Kunuk, one of the Lay Readers (later ordained and eventually made Dean of the Cathedral) and I started a men's group. We knew the women kept meeting; why couldn't the men meet as well?! We only got a very few men to start with, but that was to increase to up to 15 to 20 members later on. As we know, so many Churches consist mainly of women and a very few men. We needed to change that!

On Tuesdays during the day, I would teach some students who were preparing to be Lay Readers. I had about six people to teach and they did exceptionally well – a very willing, listening group of people. It proved to be the right thing to do for the future. They were officially recognized after the course was over. I taught two batches of people like that. I had to prepare for the teaching, so I found even Tuesdays crowded!

I do want to mention a government employee, Mike Ferris, whose son got lost and died in a blizzard. After this tragedy, I was able to make visits to him and his family and get to know them better. Later on Mike felt challenged to take a more active part in our work there – he became an official Lay Reader. Then, later still, he was ordained and did a lot to help me in the Parish. He taught others and took services, especially when I had to be away. He was an answer to my prayer, especially regarding the non-Inuit parishioners, to give them that extra help and support that I could not give. He and I worked together very well and he was a wonderful supporter of our Parish. Eventually he had to leave Iqaluit because of health problems – he was sorely missed! He has now graduated to be with his Lord in a new way.

Also on Tuesdays, every week, we had an outreach social group in the Parish Hall. It was an old building. It consisted of two old US Navy buildings from the '50s. Before my time, people had arranged for these buildings to be put together to be used as a Parish Hall. People loved that place. It was old but it was sort of cozy, and it could be used freely without worrying too much about keeping it too smart. So on Tuesday nights we arranged for Inuktitut games and Inuktitut dancing. We had one Lay Reader, Simonee Alainga, who especially helped organize this, and people just had fun. The idea was for people to get to know each other better. It is important that people who go to Church don't just see each other on a Sunday. I believe that a Church means having a real fellowship of people who love to meet together for fun and worship. It should be a place where people feel at home and uplifted. Playing games is a lot of fun, and getting families together to do this is very important – not just at Christmas time!

Margaret also realized this need for outreach to others, so she started what was called a "Mums and Tots" group for the English-speaking congregation. They would meet twice a week in our Parish Hall. It was through this group that our numbers steadily rose from the eight who we started out with in the English-speaking services at 10 o'clock, to around a hundred. They were short services and I'm sure today I'd be fired by the Bishop! This is because I cut out lengthy readings and some formal prayers and tried to vary the service as much as possible. I would make a good joke to start the sermon, and maybe also within the talk. Oddly enough I used many illustrations from the Andy Capp cartoons to make people smile and see how there's a bit of Andy in all of us. I would obviously also include an encouraging, and yet challenging message, to be a Christian and lead a Christian life. We would make sure we could have tea, coffee and cookies after that service. It was Margaret, though, who prepared all of that. At the beginning there was no one who did this with her, other than our own daughters, until a year or two after. Then people realized all that Margaret was doing and they also wanted to help. At first people just met in our Mission House, but when people grew in numbers, we had to go to the Parish Hall.

In the meantime, Margaret had to do English Sunday School in the Parish Hall before the end of the service, so she wasn't always able to be in the Cathedral whilst the service was held. Eventually others did come to help her with Sunday School, so she wasn't always doing Sunday school on a Sunday morning. Our Sunday school grew too – I would say, 60 children being taught in English under the leadership of an extremely talented teacher, Lesley Serkoak. Then there were about 80 children and youths to be taught on a Sunday afternoon in Inuktitut This was done both in the Cathedral and in some of the teachers' homes, so that the pupils would not have to go too far from their homes in winter. I had to arrange to get pictures and take-home materials to give out to the Sunday school pupils, which the Parish willingly paid for. In addition, I had to have a time to give out these materials to the teachers and prepare them for their lessons the coming Sunday. This was done during the week, as previously mentioned. We had three groups of teachers, just like we did in Pangnirtung and Kinngait.

I felt at times rather swamped by all the various things that had to be done and time to have my own preparation, my own prayers, my time with Margaret and family. These were the things that really suffered, because of all the other activities going on. It takes a while to get people involved. The whole idea is not for the Minister to do everything. He's supposed to be helping others to do things that need to be done. We don't have a dog to guard our house and then do the barking ourselves!

Then on a Wednesday we had a weekly Wednesday lunch, and this meant that some Parishioners came to the Mission House, bringing sandwiches for themselves and their family. Margaret would've made soup for everyone from leftover carcasses, chicken, turkey, ham, lamb etc. To this day I don't know how she did it! Every Wednesday she had a great vat of soup to feed 20 people or more. Our daughters also gave a lot of their leftovers for soup bones – it was a rare Wednesday when there was no Wednesday lunch! I remember though, that there was a break during mid-summer. To this day Wednesday lunches are never forgotten as it was a time of fellowship with some great food. This also was a part of the growth of our congregation in Qallunatitut (in English language).

On Thursday we had a prayer meeting in the Cathedral. We also had choir practice to go over the hymns and practice anthems for special days. The Lay Readers would get together and talk about needs or concerns, and I could teach them a little more about what we had to do to prepare for the coming Sunday in Inuktitut. I felt it was very essential to do this. I myself had to

rely upon them very much because of my lack of musical ability. I found that they were far better than me in their singing
and following hymn tunes, so that they could lead singing. We
had a wonderful organist, Pudlo, who could play by ear nearly
any hymn you'd name. We also were helped especially by a
school principal of Nakashuk School, Mungo Ireland. He would
teach a new anthem for Easter or Christmas or another special
occasion, using two-part singing. We haven't forgotten him and
to this very day so many remember his leadership and enthusiasm with thankfulness! We also had a very reliable Parishioner,
Judah, who played by ear on the organ, in the Apex Church.

Friday I tried to have free. In the morning I spent getting ready
for Sunday's sermon and prepare for any other thing that had
to be done. I still had to deal with weddings, baptisms and confirmation classes.

On Saturday, if I didn't do it on Friday, I'd have a Baptismal preparation class. Looking back, I should not have done it so close
to the actual time because they'd have the preparation on a Saturday and be baptised on the Sunday morning when there was
that special service.

I tried to involve the Lay Readers more and more on a Sunday,
so that they could sometimes preach and take part of the service. I was blessed that Brian and Rita Burrows, who had left two
years before we came to Iqaluit, had very thoroughly taught
lay people to carry on and lead services during the interregnum. They had taken over from the Rev. Don Whitbread, who
did a lot of Biblical teaching and hymn-singing training during
the time he was Incumbent there. The end result of all of this
is that, for me, it was like having several Curates to work with
ready to serve! These people really had kept things going during
the interregnum. There were people like Arnaituk, Harry, Pud-
lok and others. Then there were Simonee Alainga and Akishuk
Joamie, taking and leading services in Apex. They have all
graduated now to be with the Lord.

Counselling Ministry

One thing was really the hardest of all. When I was nicely asleep after being very tired, I'd be woken up during the night "Brr! Brr!"– that's the phone ringing! On the other end I would hear, "Mike, can you come over? I've got a problem." Now at first, I was sucked into it, and very sleepily, and most times stupidly, said yes. I would get up and go, but later on I realized that it wasn't all that worthwhile going because 90% of those who did that were drunk! I should've realized that! I should go and counsel another time, when they seemed to be sober. At first, before I better understood the situation and was "sucked in," I would go to the home at all hours of the night, talk to the person who phoned me and realize it was no use, so I would just leave without counselling and say, "I'll be back in the morning." When I went the next morning, I'd hear: "Hey Mike, what are you doing here?" Of course they had no recollection of the fight they were getting into with their wife/husband or girl/boy friend in the middle of the night when they were drunk. I was a slow learner!

Still, though, I felt I had to counsel them afterwards, to remind them about the needs of Christians not to get drunk and to help them grow in the Christian life with their families. When I first came North, I didn't realize the dangers of drink. Where we came from in England, there's a pub on every other road! When I was in England, if someone offered me a glass of wine, I wouldn't say "no." But in the North there's something about people, or rather I should say Inuit, who have less natural immunity to alcohol than non-Inuit; once they start drinking, it is very hard to stop. As I mentioned previously, the reason is that, originally, when someone caught a seal, you had to eat it all up with the neighbours and family. If you wanted to keep something for tomorrow or the day after, you'd be called a mean person. You might not actually eat it all at the feast, but anyone there at the feast would take any left-overs home, so nothing was kept back for another day. So it is still today that feeling of need to "kill the bottle." If you don't, you're mean. Then of course, because there's no inhibition after a while of taking the booze, that's where the real trouble starts – fighting, immorality, etc. It was hard and still is hard to get this message over. There is also a danger of making that alone your "Gospel message."

I mentioned before a person, Mingeriak, who helped me in Kimmirut. He had gone to Iqaluit from Kimmirut with his family for work there. When I was having to pass through Iqaluit in 1960, he came up to me and he said to me, "Mike, I have a problem with drink." I told him, "Well, you mustn't get drunk, but maybe you better quit after you've had two beers." That's the worst bit of advice I've ever given! It showed that there is no quitting after two drinks for people with alcohol problems. It is either have none, or get completely stoned! He, in the end, got so drunk that he killed his wife and a little one, whilst under the influence. That's advice I regret having given him. Eventually he jumped through a window whilst drunk and killed himself. I know that I'm forgiven for my bad counselling, but it was just being too new at things.

I know that we have to be very careful. I refrained completely from any alcohol after the first year in the North – completely refrained. Even if my family want to drink, I don't look down on them. I just hope our daughters, grandchildren and great-grandchildren, if they want to drink, will do so fully aware how it could affect other "weaker" brothers and sisters. I'm always thinking that, "Say if someone sees me drinking, they will say that 'Mike, a Minister, can drink, so can I.'" I don't want to be the cause of someone else to get an addiction, as it says in Paul's First Letter to the Corinthians 8:9: "Be careful, that the exercise of your freedom [to drink, take drugs, etc.] does not become a stumbling block to the weak." That's what was on top of my mind. I'm thankful the Lord has kept me to this promise I made when I realised the dangers to others by my drinking. I would like to see more Christian people doing the same thing, especially in this day and age when all these things are only too freely available with terrible consequences. Not that drink is a sin in itself; rather, it's the selfish misuse and abuse of it!

Then I was called out to settle disputes or to deal with a suicide, which was a most tragic thing to be called out to. It involved so much uncontrollable grief and terror for those who mourned. It involved telling many people of the tragedy and then gathering together those who could get up and go to a relative's home to cry and pray together. We knew our only comfort would come from the Lord, so we prayed together and tried to counsel the grieving relatives. I would try and get all the details I could and possibly phone relatives in other communities who would still be sleeping. Suicides always seemed to happen in the middle of the night. It was hard when you had to go out to doors and bang on them and try and get the people to open the doors, and tell them that terrible news about their loved one who had just killed himself. So many of us think it's not good to wait until the morning to tell people. They've got to know as soon as the event happens. The RCMP did open the way by dealing with the immediate relatives, but they had to concentrate more on finding out details concerning the circumstances of the suicide. The Police and myself got on well together, and I was amazed how patient and thorough I found them in these tragic situations. They even asked me to be their Chaplain, but I regretfully had to decline, as I would not have had the time to fulfil all of my obligations with them.

After all the counselling and prayers were finished, I would go home and try to get a bit of sleep, but still have to carry on some of the activities the next day that were already planned. I might cancel some activities because of a death. It was especially hard when it was on a Saturday night and there was Sunday right ahead of me! So I felt that the Lord and a lot of people gave me the strength and guidance that I needed to be able to do it all. I'm eternally thankful!

People didn't only die because of suicide. There were the usual causes of death: sickness, old age, and the longer we were in

Iqaluit, the more seemed to die of cancer. I felt inadequate to deal with all these situations, but found the Lord always provided people and words for me, which could help those grieving. I found by praying together, there was always answered prayer and a real help to those who needed that comfort.

The worst tragedy that happened was when, in the mid '80s, a group of hunters went walrus hunting down the Bay and into the open Atlantic Ocean in a Peterhead boat. They caught quite a few walrus, which meant that the boat was heavily laden. The seas got so rough that it eventually made the boat sink, together with most of its crew members. Only two survived, who had clung on to part of the floating wreckage for 48 hours in the freezing cold temperatures. The two were eventually found and brought back to Iqaluit after an experience they will never want to go through again. I assigned various Lay Readers to particular grieving families to watch over and counsel. In the end we had so many people involved and a funeral service that I never want to go through again. Bodies of the eight lost have never been recovered, and eight crosses left in our graveyard are the only visible signs left of this tragedy. The two who lived are now fine, but will never forget all that they went through.

Iqaluit Mission Weeks
In Iqaluit, we had two or three special Mission Weeks and that was a real blessing. It was at those Missions many came to the Lord. It meant a lot of preparation for potential counsellors and in planning the meetings themselves, as well as the follow-up afterwards. These Missions really, really, encouraged people and strengthened the Christian family, both in Iqaluit and others who were visiting Iqaluit from various communities.

The challenge was (and still is!) to get people to accept the Gospel and to grow and keep in the faith afterwards. Marnie Patterson was the Missioner for people in general, who had brought John Dowker along to especially work with and challenge young people with the Gospel message. John was a very gifted person who really got through to the young people there. Many accepted Christ into their lives. Unfortunately John gave up doing this work soon after he left Iqaluit, after the second Mission there. Marnie and John were both very much used by the Lord, and they were used to bring many to accept personally the Gospel message. One person comes especially to my mind who was changed by the Gospel message, and that is Nash Nowdlak. After being a real alcoholic, he saw the need to quit and has become a Lay Reader. He is very faithful in the Church, leading services and doing outreach work, especially going to BCC each week to counsel and pray with inmates there. There were many others, too numerous to comment on, who accepted Jesus as Saviour and Lord – their lives were completely changed for the better.

Dangerous and Funny Situations

I am sure that sometimes we were in real physical danger. Many times we didn't know it, other times we did! One time on a DC-3 trip going to Coral Harbour, we were told that one of the struts holding a ski used for landing on had broken. So we saw it there, hanging down in a vertical position rather than a horizontal one. The DC-3 had to land on the one remaining ski. We did! A great pilot! Another time going from Montreal to Iqaluit in a 737, the landing gear hadn't come down at all. We were wondering whether we could land or how were we going to land. The plane returned to Montreal and landed safely, but we had to first get into the crash position. You can only rely upon the Lord to be with you with His angels protecting you. I know that His promise, "I am with you always," is really true!

There was another time when someone who was a bit drunk became aggravated by his girlfriend, who had just told him she didn't want to be his girlfriend anymore. He was so mad. He came into our Mission House – that was the old Mission House -- and sat down with a loaded rifle. He was going to shoot himself and us, as he was mad at God that his girlfriend and he had just broken up. That was scary! We could only pray and do what we could do to calm him down. Margaret did what she could, which was to make tea and give him cookies! But there he was, still with his loaded, cocked rifle, just ready to pull the trigger, sitting right next to me. Margaret said that she went back to the kitchen, waiting for the gun to go off! In the end, by the grace of the Lord, he was calmed down and we got the gun from him, and it was a peaceful exit. He never got his girlfriend after that!

On a lighter note, Bible study was a weekly occurrence. To this day people still remember one slipup that I made when I was starting Bible study with a group of parishioners there. I said, "We're going to have Bible study tonight, I welcome you," but the word that I used in Inuktitut for Bible Study, I missed out a syllable. Igjujuit is the Inuktitut for what Inuit called the New Testament in those days. Igjuk is the word for testicle. So I said by accident, "We're now going to have testicle study" rather than my saying "Bible study." Of course that made everyone burst out with laughter. But that's the sort of thing we can laugh at, and that's not taken as a bad thing, it just made the Bible study more interesting!

Then there were other times I went to bless houses with ghosts or evil spirits in them. I really am sure that it's not all imagination and there are evil beings. As St. Paul says: "We are not fighting just against human beings, but against spiritual forces and cosmic powers of this dark age" (Ephesians 6: 12). There are definitely evil influences, and even demons, and we don't realize it until very unnatural ghostly, unexplainable things happen. Again, I felt very inadequate. I could only just truly trust the Lord to hear our prayer. I would go with at least one other person, and we would have a short opening prayer in the home there. Then we would have a prayer in each room of the house with the family. We prayed that any evil would go and the Lord Jesus would truly reign there in that home and in peoples' hearts – and He did! That was a real reassurance to me, how the Lord listens to us whenever we have to earnestly pray to Him.

I would still have to go around with Bishop Sperry on his visitations to various Parishes. One thing I didn't really like was small planes. One time he had arranged to go visiting and had chartered a plane. When I stood up by the plane I could look over the top of it! It was so funny (in retrospect). He tried to stop me from thinking too much about being scared in a small plane – so he'd bring his chess set along, because we were great competitors in chess, one trying to outwit the other. When I was on that tiny plane I would look down on the mountains below – they seemed so rugged and vast – we were so tiny and frail! This all made me not able to concentrate on the game, as I was so busy looking for possible landing sites – more than looking for landing sites for my Queen to get on to, in order to checkmate him. At least that was my excuse for losing!

Bishop Sperry awaits me to pluck up courage and board our "fancy plane!"

Another time he got me going to Igloolik because he said I must go, as the Roman Catholic congregation there wanted to make a presentation to me. He said that they were very thankful that I was able to visit patients from there who had to stay in the hospital in Iqaluit. They wanted to thank me by giving me something. So I went there with him and we had a service with speeches afterwards. It seemed a big to-do just before this presentation. When the time came, there it was, a tiny little carving, about two inches high! I didn't want to look down on it, but we were bad and chuckled about how he had thought it would be a big carving. It was the thought that was much appreciated, coming from the Roman Catholics there. The carving was of a bird with a long neck. Eventually, I'm afraid, the neck got broken and I had to glue it up to make it whole. Whenever I look at it, it makes me chuckle!

Future Replacements and a New Parish Hall

It was getting closer to the time that I thought I should be retiring. The question came up about my replacements. It was arranged that the Reverends Louie Mike and Daniel Aopaluk would come to run the Parish. The Very Rev Roger Briggs came later. There were various other ordained and lay people, who also came later. It seemed that we needed a lot of people to carry on all the activities that we had been doing. Also, I should mention, my retirement project was to make sure there was a better Parish Hall for the growing numbers of parishioners. The total cost of this came around to $740,000. We had a wonderful committee to work out all the details of ordering and constructing the building – let alone fund raising! It got built by many people helping and pulling together under the leadership of the committee's Chairman, Chris Groves.

It was in December of 1995 when it actually opened. Our new Parish Hall was such a blessing to have after our small old Parish Hall. We found, however, that there was some loss of intimacy that was possible with the snugness of the old Parish Hall. People there had been close together. We loved the openness and cleanliness of the new Hall, but at first, a bigger Hall meant the people seemed to be more apart, to be not so close in fellowship. As time went on we all got to treasure our new

Parish Hall that seemed so large and clean after the old one. We realised what a blessing that there was a Parish Hall which was larger, because in 2005 the Cathedral burnt down and then we had no place of worship, except to use the new Parish Hall. So people went there instead for worship on Sundays. It was harder though, because you couldn't do two activities at the same time in the one building. Prior to the Cathedral being burnt down, you could have a service in the Cathedral, and at the same time have related activities in the Parish Hall. However I didn't really get involved too much with that new situation of arranging Parish activities. I got a little pressure from my family to be reminded that I'm retired, but I know that we never get to be fully retired! Whatever we can do for the Lord, whether we're clergy or not, whatever age we are, we should do all with His strength and help.

CHAPTER 6:
RETIREMENT

Retirement Thoughts And Events

In 1996 I was getting on in years and Margaret's health wasn't the greatest because she'd been burdened with arthritis and congenital heart disease. She became more reliant upon me, and with all of this Parish work going on I just couldn't do both -- being there as a husband as much as I should be, and father and grandfather to my family. So when I got to the age of 65, I felt that I needed to retire and just to help in the background where necessary.

Margaret had looked after me for many years, so it was my turn to look after her! So I had to push the button and say that I should retire. That was in April. When this became known, parishioners kindly worked on giving me a great retirement party. There were so many well-wishes and prayers. It meant so much to us. We had a book of personalised cartoons about life after retirement given to us, all based on my favourite cartoon character – Andy Capp. I even had a special autographed cartoon, framed, direct from the creator of Andy Capp – Reg Smythe. That was amazing! Then there were special messages and gifts from the parishioners, which included a little hand-made book from the Sunday School children. All are remembered and deeply treasured. (I am happy that we were able to bring all these special items with us to Ottawa). One of my Andy Capp local cartoons showed a great vat of soup on the table, enough for 20 people, at our Wednesday lunches, but there was only Margaret and me to have it all! The comment was, "Margaret forgot that you're retired!" Here is an Andy Capp-style local cartoon:

Another cartoon was about how I had, in the past, a race with all the parents of children in Sunday School. Amazingly I won over them all in that race! That cartoon reminded me of that happy time when so many from the Church enjoyed family fun and fellowship together. We need that warmth still today!

Then I also received a huge retirement present of $5,000 – people knew I needed a new snowmobile, so that went towards buying me one. That was in the springtime at the end of April. Margaret and I then went on holiday to try to sort of recover and get refreshed again. We had a good second honeymoon, going to England and Jersey. The latter is one of the Channel Islands. It was interesting to see all the remains of the German occupation there. Yes! The Germans did occupy part of English soil! Since retirement we've been to Bermuda and Hawaii. Then in 2002, with all the family, we went again to the UK. We had a great time there in London, Newquay and Worcester. Imagine us all packed into, and going around in, a great big van which son-in-law Archie drove. He had a challenging time trying to negotiate left hand driving and the roundabouts in England. We also have never forgotten about how one Sunday we went to a country Church in Crantock, near Newquay. It happened to be a Baptismal service as well as Communion. The Minister had only brought the water in a gin bottle – and he wasn't sure how much was gin and how much was water! It was also a very high Anglo-Catholic Church and they used incense. My family laughed at me as I couldn't stop sneezing, because the incense got up my nose! We also spent a lot of the time on the beautiful Newquay sands, swimming and surfing in the sea. We will never forget that holiday. I'm very thankful we could have it together as a family. So important to be able to celebrate together! It's great to have a holiday, just the "Old Folks" together, but even better when we can have our family with us.

It's hard to retire, especially when you're staying in the same place that you were working in. People do still think you're not retired and say on the phone, "Can you come? We've got ghosts in our house. Can you come and give a blessing for the house?" I always said, "I will come, but you must first consult with the Minister (at that time Jonas Allooloo) as I'm not in charge. If he can't make it I will go. Anyway I will check with you later to see how things went." Oddly enough it quite often happened that the Minister asked me to go; indeed it was nice to still be able to go and visit people with a real goal in mind. I never have any regrets about having retired in Iqaluit, because I knew the people and I still could do things rather than be put out to pasture!

Our New House and Family
In 1991, I was able to build a house for us to live in. We had been

living in the Mission House in Iqaluit since 1981. It's a sort of tithed house – that means that you can only live in it if you're working. Being retired, you're not working anymore, so it was a real blessing that we could have a house of our own – a house for Margaret, Kym and myself. Our three daughters had gone off, leaving the nest to find and marry their future partners. They lived elsewhere as a result.

Even before I had retired, Ann had gone to Grise Fiord on Ellesmere Island and was living there. Pat was in Iqaluit with her husband Archie, and Sue was in Almonte, Ontario living with her husband there, until later returning to Iqaluit to work.

The house we got was ideal and it was an answer to a prayer. We had to get a site for it and that was a challenge in Iqaluit in 1991. Because all land in town was under land claim negotiation, available lots were controlled by the town. We had got a site allocated to us which we really didn't like. It was in the middle of a lot of commotion and traffic. But then, suddenly, another site became available and there were two of us who wanted it: a Department of Transport person and ourselves. I have no idea who the DOT person was. Our next-door neighbours-to-be, Moe and Mikalee Lewis, they really prayed that we would get that site. Behold! The City Council did agree that we were the ones to have it! It was a very nice site overlooking the sea by the beach. This would mean you could see people and cars going along an informal beach road, as well as planes landing at the airport. Then there were ships unloading supplies onto barges, which would then come in to unload on the special sealift beach near us. Then there were all the beautiful snow-capped mountains in the distance to look at. As the years went by, more and more people used that beach road and it became quite a main road, as it's a shortcut to avoid all the traffic congestion at 8 o'clock, 12 o'clock and 5 o'clock. Rush hour had finally come to Iqaluit!

We were blessed that a contractor named Bill said he would build our house, and the only thing we had to pay for was the labour to build the house. All the materials were provided

under the home ownership program of the NWT Government (this was before the creation of Nunavut). That home owner- ship program was a wonderful one for people like ourselves! Un- fortunately that program was cut off after the next year, so it is much more difficult and costly to get a house since the time that we got ours. Our house was a three-bedroom bungalow. It being a bungalow turned out to be a blessing for later on, when Margaret was confined to a wheelchair. We also had a ramp put in for that house so Margaret could be wheeled in and out of the house more easily.

Our own Iqaluit house looking out over Frobisher Bay (Picture courtesy of Susan Gardener)

Kym is a changed person for the better now. He lived with us for a few years after we moved into our new house, and helped us settle down into that house. Unfortunately he got into bad company, and it was very hard to have him there. We were left with no choice but that of his leaving us. The original plan, when he was four years old, was that he would only be staying with us for four months – still there 30 years later! It made us learn how hard it is, or was, to be a teenager in Iqaluit. So many of the teenagers are influenced by their peer groups. They were the ones who drank, smoked pot and engaged in wild living.

It made me realize what a great need to continue to have a true

Christian young peoples' group. In 1998 I had given up running our youth group, the Northern Lights. I felt I was getting beyond it. I was able to get a couple to lead the group, who had been Northern Lights members themselves, when they were a bit younger. They were Jimmy and Moosee. I had taken the marriage service for them in the '80s. They took on the Northern Lights leadership and did a good job. They arranged many activities, Bible activities and games, and even took young people on camping expeditions and to meetings held in other communities. But unfortunately after about three years, various situations came about to make it that they could not carry on the great work that they were doing. It was hard to find a successor, so the Northern Lights group eventually stopped running. The original members still communicate with each other, and I'm very happy about that.

Later on we had a Church Army Captain, Ron McLean and his wife Carol, who came to help the Parish out. He was eventually ordained in Iqaluit and put in charge of the Parish. Ron McLean was very instrumental in starting up the soup kitchen, which was meant to be an outreach program. This soup kitchen is still running to this day, although it is now run mainly by the City and not so much by the Church, although it's on Church property. Mike Ferris and Russ Blanchette (a Church Army Captain who came later on) also helped a lot to keep the soup kitchen up and running. I had another project that I wanted to do. That was to have a Church Bookroom. There was our golden opportunity! Ron's wife had had past experience in that sort of thing; also Russ had had a lot of business experience before becoming a Church Army Captain. These two took a major role in getting it going, together with the help of others, and there was the new Parish Hall. We could use one of its rooms as a Bookroom. People could now buy Christian books and supplies in both languages right there in Iqaluit! This was a necessary and successful venture.

Just to add a word about a special event for me that I feel should be mentioned. That was in 2007, when I was told that I had been awarded the Order of Canada. That really shook me! When we were about to receive the medal I was with all the other recipients, and it made me feel very "little" compared with all that they had done. I however felt that I had to accept the honour –so our whole family went to Ottawa to meet the Governor General. It was a memorable occasion. I felt that I should cut the medal into three – one third to Margaret, one third to my daughters and the other third to me! In 2011, I was also given the Order of Nunavut. I am always reminded as part of an old prayer that goes "we have no power ourselves to help ourselves." It is only by the grace of God can we have lives that can help others.

Tragedy Strikes the Cathedral
In 2005, tragedy struck. A guy who, it is said, wanted to worship Satan, came one Saturday night in the fall of 2005 and had poured gas in the interior of the Cathedral in three places and set it alight. The first I knew of it was when our daughter Sue phoned to say, "Hurry up! there's smoke coming out of the Cathedral!" So I ran there and went to look to see what was going on and, lo and behold, yes, there was smoke pouring out of the outside porch doors! We just could only stay and look at it and wait for the fire brigade to come. Whilst we were looking, there was a lady, who we didn't know, encouraged us by saying, "Don't worry, it will be rebuilt!" We couldn't find her anywhere afterward – that was some mysterious person. Was it an angel reassuring us? As we now know, the Cathedral was a write-off. The destruction was too much. The only answer was to build a new Cathedral. Consequently, a lot of fundraising work was done to raise money to build this new Cathedral. At first there were fancy blueprints that we didn't agree with, to make a building something like the Sydney Opera House, but they were toned down instead to be the great building that we now have. The rebuilt Cathedral was opened in 2012. This was only possible because of a lot of fundraising, causing no end of "blood, sweat

and tears" with all the effort that had to be made over the years to raise sufficient millions for the new building. We were all especially thankful to the Fundraising Committee under the leadership of Ed Picco, who were able to "close shop" at the end of 2017, when all the necessary $10 million had been raised – what a cause for celebration!

At the time of writing this our old friend, the Rev. Methusalah Kunuk, is now in charge of the Parish as Dean of the Cathedral. His recently ordained wife, Martha, is also helping in the work. A young married couple, Jared and Rebecca, came to help things out in Iqaluit but have now been transferred to Rankin Inlet. Joey Royal, who was the Principal of ATTS in Iqaluit, has now been consecrated as Bishop, so this new position will often take him away from Iqaluit. It is a shame that when clergy get established in a key place, they then get moved while they are doing a great job. It is still important not to be just another southerner who quickly comes and goes, without ever having the chance to be a real part of the community and being able to get fully immersed in Inuit culture.

St. Jude's Anglican Church in Iqaluit (Photo Credit: Cwk36~commonswiki)

Inside St. Jude's Cathedral after it had just opened in June 2012

Move to Ottawa

So we're thankful the way the Lord has been with us to have made Margaret, my family and myself feel at home in Iqaluit. It was only Margaret's medical conditions, which included advancing dementia, that made it imperative for us to have to leave Iqaluit. We had to go to where she could get better nursing care – there were no facilities in Nunavut at all for her and others with more than Stage 1 dementia. I was handed a letter dated April 7, 2016, from her doctor in Iqaluit which said "Mrs. Gardener was admitted to hospital two days ago with congestive heart failure. Her condition has deteriorated, and unfortunately she is not expected to survive. Her life expectancy, I believe is measured in days." That letter was like a bombshell to me. I immediately contacted Ann and Kym, so that we could all be together as a family (Sue and Pat were already in Iqaluit). We got others to pray for her, that the doctor's verdict would be wrong – and it was!

GARDENER, MARGARET

CASE HISTORY & PROGRESS NOTES

April 7th, 2016

To Whom it may concern:

Mrs. Gardener was admitted to hospital 2 days ago c̄ Congestive Heart Failure. Her condition has deteriorated and, unfortunately, she is not expected to survive. Her life expectancy, I believe, is measured in days

Respectfully, Clay Marco, MD

(Marco)

GN1485/1003 F52/1003

Two weeks later she was medevacked to Ottawa. It was extremely hard for us to leave people we loved, knew and cared for, and move to a new situation and live in an Elders' facility, the Embassy West Senior Living (EWSL) in Ottawa. It's been hard to make the change, but we know we have to do this. It is rather like culture shock in reverse! Margaret is getting the care she needs for her mind and body. In fact, now people who visit her here, and have known her in Iqaluit, all say that they have never seen her looking as good as this for a long time! It is still very hard to accept how, mentally, she's a different person from what she used to be. She has always been an amazing partner! We give thanks to the Lord for His guidance. At this time we can think back and reflect on some of the special things that have happened in the past, and be thankful that we were chosen to do this particular work together.

CONCLUDING REMARKS

On the Future of Nunavut: Government and Church

I want to talk a little about how I see the future for Nunavut for both government and Church.

As far as government goes, I myself am happy that it is a non-partisan government, although there are advantages and disadvantages for this. I know from my own personal experience that the government in Nunavut is more directed by middle and senior management and deputy ministers than the actual MLAs. It does not matter who you vote for, as Ministers on the whole have little power to change things. Some Ministers even do not want to make changes and rubber-stamp policies and statements written and given to them by the bureaucrats. If Ministers do want to make changes, they have to be "in league" with policy makers, lawyers and other bureaucratic staff. MLAs and some Ministers find that most of their ideas are squashed by the bureaucrats in their department, who want to keep to the status quo. I believe that is also mainly true of the Feds as well. There's also a danger of each MLA only thinking of his or her constituents rather than the whole of Nunavut. As long as that carries on it's going to be hard for the whole of Nunavut to grow.

The future lies in getting those MLAs who will be willing to go out on a limb for the good of all of Nunavut, to work hard to get new projects, and positively beneficial policies, going. Also each MLA and Minister must have the guts to deal with a lot of nastiness, negativity and personal rivalry from within the bureaucracy and some Ministers. Then you've always got the tension between commercializing natural resources and the way this process interferes with hunting, fishing and the rights of the people who were first here, the Inuit.

I myself as a father am so thankful for my own daughter Pat, who as an elected member of the Nunavut Legislative Assembly worked extremely hard to help her constituents. When there is no actual impetus from the government as a whole to do something about a bad situation in Nunavut, she is not afraid to speak out (as long as it is not a family matter to make a conflict of interest!). The best example of this was her determination to have a dementia care facility available in Nunavut, so that Nunavummiut do not have to go south to Ottawa to be cared for when they have dementia. There are more and more people who are getting dementia, and there are going to be more people needing extra care because of the bad results from an increasing abuse of drugs and alcohol. I see that as an unfortunate part of the future. As each year goes by there is an increasing need for a suitable facility in Nunavut. My daughter Pat overcame many obstacles from some bureaucrats who, for some of their own vested reasons, wanted to make it hard to have an Elder's Centre for dementia care in Iqaluit. Their opposition was more for their own commercial benefit – making it a private company, rather than a non-profit group running it. I'm afraid my view of the future is that there will always be these people who want to do things for their own benefit and not for the good of the whole.

Then there are commercial outfits, some of which gouge Nunavummiut. One example of this is NorthMart (read-The North-

West Company) selling water for $2 or more a bottle, when you can get 24 of those same bottles for $2 in the south. Another example was one Co-op store selling a watermelon for $75! Unless people have good government jobs, they find it a real struggle to make ends meet. In fact, as one CBC Marketplace program stated, 75% of Nunavut children have gone to bed hungry. I believe Christians should speak out more about these matters, and I am hoping that by the time this book is published, a lot of these "gouging issues" will have been solved. The Government can and must step in to legislate, to put a cap on the high cost of basic items, so that even those on Social Assistance will be able to buy basic food and sanitary items. Or am I too naive to wish that? I hope not!

The high cost of living will always be in Nunavut, because of distance and transportation cost. There will be a greater gap between those who are well off and those who are poor. Besides the problems of food security for all, there will also always be the problems of housing, health, education and learning to budget wisely the money that a family has.

We need, to my mind, to stop making it just Inuit who are considered available for the jobs ahead. It's got to be any person who is a genuine long-term resident of Nunavut, to be considered for employment. Hiring should be by ability rather than race! At the present time, "southerners" come up North who do have good skills, stay a little to earn lots of money, and then go back south. Whilst in the North they are given a lot of responsibility, but they provide answers and recommend actions that are not "northernized." They are called experts and have a lot of power. Often it is a friend who knows a friend that is hired. I see that unless that is stopped, it's going to be even a greater problem in the future. We have to have people who truly love and want to live in Nunavut to lead it, regardless of race. My prayer of course is that this will be a reality, as the government gets more concerned about the whole of Nunavut, rather than just a part. All Nunavummiut should have equal say in things and equal opportunities. Being a Christian, I believe, means that we are very concerned about all of these matters. I believe it clearly shows in the New Testament how Jesus got angry when there was inequality and racial prejudices – so should we!

As far as the Christian Faith goes, I look back, before looking to the future, to be thankful for all the work that has continued to these days, because of past missionaries who came to the Arctic for the sake of the Gospel. They taught Inuit, who in turn taught others, who also became missionaries. Their efforts and those they have taught have not been in vain, and we owe a huge debt to them for all they did. Now it's up to us!

So many social issues have caused some people to no longer take much notice of what the New Testament teaches. It is now a humanistic society. When we first went to Kimmirut there was almost 100% Church attendance. Compare that now with Iqaluit, with all the Churches put together, you'd be very lucky to get 400 people on any Sunday - unless it's Christmas. That is less than five percent of the whole population. That is below the national average. So something has happened over the years. It is also, as we know, a trend in the south. The Christian Church as a whole needs much more cooperation among the various denominations, and not to avoid those who worship differently.

I myself do not believe that we should pray to the Saints, as Jesus has said to pray direct to the Father through Him. I do not believe that we should shout at God and demand that He do something right away to heal someone, like you see some TV evangelists doing. I believe we build up a relationship with Jesus day by day, putting everything into His hands and trusting that He is always with us. That is the true way for peace. The basic message of the Gospel is the knowledge that we are saved, not by our good works but by faith alone. Knowing that fact, this makes us want to lead a Christian life, however poorly we do this! Churches must not get into a dull routine of long-winded dry sermons and speeches. The services of the future must be uplifting and be thankful for the love that God has for each one of us.

I believe that the Church will go forward. In fact out of all of the Anglican Churches, those in the Arctic, I'm sure, will be the ones that will survive the longest, compared with so many Anglican churches in the South. When I go to a Church I often think, if I was non-Christian, would that service inspire me enough to want to be a Christian? Would I want to go back again next week? Or if I'm a young person, would it be too ritualistic and lengthy and boring to make me want to go again to that particular Church?

I know the Gospel has been fully preached in the North. I know it does fall on many deaf ears because of drugs, alcoholism, violence, unresolved conflicts and immoral living – but that doesn't mean we give up! We're still called to be missionaries for Jesus even in this 21st century – that calling never, never finishes.

Although attendance numbers are down, I believe the so-called "decline" is because those who do go to Churches today are going because they really want to go, leaving out many who, in the past, just went along with the crowd without any personal commitment. Indeed, statistically, this will mean fewer people who go. The so-called falloff is only in numbers, not in quality. If I go to the zoo, by the fact of going, it does in no way make me an ape. So just by the fact of going to Church, it does not make me a Christian! Another reason, I believe, for the falloff in the North is because of full-time jobs during the week. Many more people have full-time employment now than those who lived in the fifties and sixties. Those who have full-time employment can only get off work on the weekend. That means going away to go hunting or camping or fishing. So people who would go to Church miss it – it does not mean they are not Christian. So the Church attendance numbers do not give us a true picture. It is true also that, for some, there's not just the will to go to Church, but to play sports and do other things, even when in the community. We forget that Church is like a hospital for forgiven sinners – like me!

In the future, there's going to be more and more full-time employment, mining projects and things like that. When one parent has to be away from the home for frequent duty tours, it will affect the unity and faith of families, unless both parents are truly committed Christians. I see it will be a real challenge to lead a committed Christian life – the only answer is to have families practicing their Christian faith, with their children involved as well. We need to have informal Church events for the whole family during the middle of the week (like the new movement called "The Messy Church") for people who go away at the weekend. We need more emphasis on youth, and have special services for young people. This is all so important! I see the necessity to think out a new way how the clergymen and congregation could be doing more of for the future of the Church in Iqaluit, and indeed anywhere in Nunavut. We need committed Christian leaders who know the language and the North very well, who preach and teach the Gospel by their actions as well as by their words: people who will get out to meet and welcome new people, visit their homes, and encourage them to come to Church and grow in their Christian Faith. I hope our Churches in the North will be Churches without walls, as it were. Nunavut is a wonderful place and it is especially wonderful when we have people there who truly follow the Lord in their daily lives.

Final Thoughts

I do want to recognize all those past missionaries who worked in the Diocese of the Arctic and trained lay people to spread the Gospel, right from the time of the first missionary who went to Baffin Island, the Reverend Peck. He made many converts and those he taught also made many converts. Mr. Peck did an enormous amount of translating work, putting the Moravian Scriptures that were in roman orthography into syllabics, as well as making them more Baffin Island dialect-friendly. He also produced some teaching materials and hymns in syllabics. In this way it was possible for all the Inuit in their isolated camps to be able to read and understand the Scriptures without having to have clergy on hand all the time. Most of the material was based on the New Testament. I believe this was another strength of missionary work – people were not confused by trying to understand all the books of the Old Testament. I believe that we should only study these books of the Old Testament in the light of the New Testament. The whole Bible has now been put into syllabics by the hard work of many Inuit translators under the sponsorship of the Canadian Bible Society. I am amazed that today we have the full Inuktitut Bible and many teaching materials at our finger tips, yet often neglect to study them!

It is much harder now than it used to be, to live a life fully committed to the Christian Faith, and have a daily prayerful relationship with the Lord Jesus. It's harder than before because of all the many distractions to keep us busy – sports, movies, Internet, finances, Facebook, etc. In the past, life was very hard for many in the North with poverty, hunger, sickness and so on, but in all of this, people were more aware of their weakness and need for daily dependence on the Lord. There are indeed some very committed Christian people today, who are desperate to learn all what it means to follow the Lord. They will carry on through thick and thin, in spite of all the obstacles and various activities that try to sidetrack them. It means, however, that those who are less committed are more easily swayed to go their own way. So I do see the future of the Church in the Arctic to be solid and assured, because it is still based on God's Word much more than you may find in some Anglican Churches in the south. I am also very happy that St. Stephen's Anglican Church, which we go to in Ottawa, is Bible-based and has a good message and outreach to the community. It also has a good mixture of modern hymns as well as the more traditional ones. Also the whole service is projected onto the wall, so you do not have to worry about finding pages and the right book. I would like to see this idea in all Churches in the North, but it involves a lot of work and some extra expenses.

There are many different religions, customs etc. coming up North, more than ever before. I pray that those who are loyal to the Christian faith and Bible will not be swamped, or want to put their Christian faith on the "back-burner." My prayer is that Christians in the North will remain united in continuing to lead a Christian life, encouraging others to do so, regardless of other new, non-Christian teachings.

I also pray that those who look at pre-Christian days with rose tinted spectacles will not be hoodwinked in to thinking that these past ways of living are more to be desired than Christian ones. A few who think this and blame missionaries for getting rid of a lot of these customs and culture are really looking at the past in a very unrealistic way. We forget how much Christianity has to be thanked for getting rid of many taboos, people living in fear of offending spirits or the local shaman, and a lot of hardship just to survive. It should also be noted how pre-Christian lives for women were especially hard, concerning taboos about menstruating and childbirth (being put in an igloo on their own as untouchables) and the way they were harshly treated by their husbands. We must not forget how the early missionaries strived with a lot of opposition to get the message of the Christian Gospel over. This opposition was because the Gospel message went against those who had power in pre-Christian days. The Gospel message did indeed, rightfully, change many old customs that would not be accepted today. We must not forget that it was Christian people who first brought hospitals and health care to the Inuit. The Gospel brought, and still does bring, the need to give all women full respect and have equal rights with men (of course, men have to have equal rights as well). The problems of today are not caused by the fact of people no longer having and following their past culture, but rather, are caused by those who no longer listen to or practice the New Testament teachings of the Lord.

I'm not a prophet but I do know that because of so many southern influences, it will be harder to keep true to the Christian way of living than it was 50 years ago. There are so many non-Christian influences that are increasingly coming to the North to cause confusion. An obvious example is the increasing availability of alcohol and drugs, more family violence and the mix-up of various cultures and even non-Christian religions. Another issue that was never outwardly there 50 years ago is that of same-sex relationships and how the Church stands on this issue. There is still tension between those who want to go hunting on a Sunday and those who will not hunt then. A lot of people in the south don't see any reason why you shouldn't go hunting then, whilst this offends some others in the North. Another example is with alcohol - it's no big deal in the south to have a beer, but in the North it becomes an issue and there's a danger of the south swamping the North with ideas that the North is not ready for.

These differences of opinion and customs can only be worked out when there's mutual understanding and having Christian charity of thought in all these issues – yet remaining strong in our Christian ways. So there are many situations which have to be solved, but working together as a Christian family of people who follow the Lord, then I know these problems will be worked through, although they'll never will be fully solved.

Margaret's Contribution to Our Missionary Work in the Arctic

I do again want to acknowledge Margaret, my lovely wife, who has done so much. Without her support, I don't know where we would have been. Indeed she deserved the award she got in 2014 to be the recipient of the Wise Woman Award from Qulliit Nunavut Status of Women Council. She has done so much! Besides looking after three daughters, a foster son and myself, she has taught Sunday School, ran a Mums and Tots group, and counselled community members in their times of need when I wasn't there. She has helped and taught Catechists' wives, Lay Readers' wives, Ordinands' wives, teaching them what it means to be a wife in a Parish. She also, when in Pangnirtung, ran GA (Girls' Auxiliary) and JA (Junior Auxiliary) groups. In her "spare time" she loved to knit and made many little knitted dolls for Church Sales – these are treasured to this day! Could anyone do all these things, and in addition have a full-time job which takes that person out of their house for most of the day? We know the answer! I was old-fashioned and knew that we could survive on one salary alone. In this way, Margaret could always be there keeping the home fires burning, and be very much more in Parish life, keeping in touch with people and helping with the various groups. Margaret was like an unpaid Executive Secretary monitoring the phone (no cell phones then) and with her impeccable organization skills, she directed me to various Parish needs and kept me on the right track. I am convinced that by her being so willing and available to give help to people, that our Parish grew from strength to strength. There is a weakness today when there is nobody in the Mission House/Rectory. If the Parish gives a sufficient allowance for housing, I know that it is possible for the spouse to be a non-wage earner at home who could fulfill this important role in the Church. If this is not possible there must be a paid (or volunteer) Secretary to help organise Parish life. Margaret also took services whilst I've been away - and that's many times –and she has looked after the running of our house. She has had to deal with angry, suicidal people, who barged into our house, as well as serving tea and cookies to people who wanted just to visit.

When you think of it, she was a woman taken from the middle of England right out to the Arctic, then, many times, left alone with herself and just two or three little girls. It's amazing what she did – we know the Lord Himself gave her the strength!

To look after all of us she had to spend a lot of time cooking, which especially in the earlier days, when we first went to the North, was not an easy job. Then there was no store to buy anything from, so she had to do things herself and make items our family needed. As our little family got a little older, things were harder. She had to make six loaves at least twice a week, plus baking cookies and cooking the meals and trying to make meals out of not too much! But she did it. She did it, maybe, with just dehydrated potato, dried vegetable flakes and a roast of fish or something like that. She did it in a cheerful way and got to know the people of the communities and entertained them and even invited tourists for supper – and so much more – I cannot do justice in this book to relate all that she's done.

At this point I should also recall the fact that Margaret became riddled with arthritis as well as heart problems. Because of her arthritis, after her hysterectomy operation she had to eventually have both knee joints replaced, one hip joint replaced and a very intensive operation to remove 7" of her small intestine that had become twisted. Yet after all these operations and stays in hospitals she still carried on with Parish work!

Now she is in Ottawa, because she has dementia. We won't understand why until we come to be with the Lord. Yes, indeed I'm thankful for the support Margaret gave me, all the things she did and no woman in the south of Canada was willing to do at that time. In the '50s and '60s any potential missionary wives who came up North with their husbands seemed to go back south as quickly as possible, when they saw the living conditions in the Mission House and community that they would be in.

I do want to thank our three daughters Ann, Sue and Pat for their support of Margaret and me over the years. They were brought up in sparse surroundings in our home and with very basic food. They survived school days which must have been very hard for them – non-Inuit kids were not always made welcome by teachers, by regional NWT Government, or even by some fellow pupils. They also had to be uprooted from their home and sent south for schooling, because the NWT Government did not provide schooling beyond Grade 6 at that time. I am proud of my daughters who survived all of this and now are well-established in good positions with the Nunavut government. Our three daughters are always helping us two old folks! I'm thankful they all found good jobs and have a home of their own with their own families. We always pray for them and their families. I'm also thankful that all my nine grandchildren have secured jobs with homes and families. That is an achievement these days! And I'm thankful that Kym has now turned over a completely new leaf and has settled down to live here in Ottawa. He came to realize his old life of booze and wild living was not the way, and I'm deeply thankful he's changed.

Margaret and myself with: Ann, Pat, me, Susan and Kym (from L to R)

My Life's Message

So my dear family, friends and readers, I pray that you will take

Jesus for real, that He is living today and is a reality for eternity! He wants you to be with Him. Have Him as your true Saviour and Lord as the only way to heaven. You may get turned off by Christians talking about the reality of sin. If we feel like this, we have to answer the question, why would Jesus go through all that suffering and dying on the cross if there was no need to save us from sin and false teaching? Not everyone does go to heaven. There is no such thing as a "cross-less Christianity." There is such a thing as sin and the need to be saved. We don't usually realize this until maybe later on in life and I pray you will come to acknowledge this fact yourself.

I don't understand why so many don't really believe in and trust Jesus as a real historical person, fully God and, of course, living today and into eternity. Many people saw Him after His resurrection and knew He was for real. Many were persecuted when they professed their faith in the risen Christ and would never waiver even under the threat of death. They could do this because they knew Jesus to be real and living within them still today. There are many who have near-death experiences and meet Him. This fact, from many who have these experiences, also proves Jesus to be true and undeniable. There are many things in our faith that we don't understand. If we could fully understand everything about God and His ways, then our God would be too small! Let us trust that which we do know, and follow the historical reality of a risen Christ and an indwelling Holy Spirit – trust that we are forgiven sinners and accepted by God for eternity. We need to have a daily personal relationship with Jesus that stretches right into eternity!

That is the Gospel message and I prayerfully hope we can all accept it. There is no other way.

Looking back on my own spiritual journey I realize how God knows us so much, as if there is only one to know. He can arrange for our future and will guide us along the future path as long as we are willing to accept His guidance and His will. His will is not always what we think it is and His timing is different and more flexible than ours. As I said earlier, when I first got my calling I was 12-years-old. I agreed to go to the Arctic. However, looking back I realise that I agreed to go for a wrong reason. I thought what I would do - "do" is the emphatic word! I thought that what I could do would get me into heaven and be a way to get accepted by God. It was only much later around the age of 19 (I can't place a day or time) I had a special realization moment of knowing what the Christian faith truly is. I don't believe all of us have to have that one special moment of sudden realization. It can be gradual and people come into our lives to help make it to be a reality. When I was in the Air Force, a Scripture Reader (as they were called) came and talked to me and helped me realize that we are saved by trusting Jesus and accepting Him into our hearts and lives. It is not what we do. It is what He has done for us! He alone, as the hymn says, "could unlock the door of heaven and let us in" to go to heaven after we die and know we already have eternal life that we were given when we accepted Jesus as Saviour and Lord into our own lives. We need to have a relationship with Jesus here and now, a continuing relationship here on earth, trusting Him. I'm not saved by what I can do but by what He has done on the cross for me already!

That's the foundation of my life and I pray it will be a foundation for your life also. In Ephesians chapter 2, verse 8, it says, "It is by God's grace that you have been saved through faith. It is not the result of your own efforts." That's true, but then after realizing we have been saved by Jesus dying for us, then we want to be thankful, then we want to show forth our thankfulness, to do what we can for His sake. This was all a great new message to me and I still want to make it new every day. I pray that all my family and those reading these words will come to accept this and lead a life truly accordingly, wherever they are working or living. I was the most unlikely candidate to be sent to the Arctic! However God never gave up on me, but instead worked in me to provide what I needed to stay and minister in the Arctic. He also did that for Margaret. I believe He will truly do this for you also, when you want Jesus in your life and heart as Saviour and Lord. He wants to win your heart to Him. You can serve Him wherever you are – obviously you do NOT have to be an ordained Minister or go to the Arctic to do this! You can serve Him wherever you are. Whatever happens we must accept His leading. There are so many who need His light to shine into their lives, and He so often uses us for this to happen!

The whole purpose of this book is to show that He can take you or me, however much an unlikely candidate we may seem to be (like I was and still am!). He can come and live in us and start a relationship that will last for eternity.

I close with the prayer I love most, as part of a continuing relationship with Jesus:

Lord Jesus, Loving Saviour, Friend and Brother

May I know You more clearly,

Love You more dearly,

And follow You more nearly,

This day and every day into eternity

Amen.

(Prayer based on the prayer of St. Richard of Chichester)

* * *

ACKNOWLEDGEMENTS

I wish to acknowledge with real thanks all those who have helped me to get the various items together for this memoir:

John MacDonald, who put me on the right track for recording my thoughts and getting them transcribed. There were so many technical details that he solved for me. His encouragement, knowledge and patience with me were amazing! He is still continuing to take the necessary steps for this book to be published.

Hassan, who worked at the Embassy West, for all his help in consolidating and arranging the first transcribed text on my computer.

For our granddaughter-in-law Tara Angnakak's help with map illustrations and arranging pictures and formatting text for the final draft

Sharon Angnakak, our granddaughter, who encouraged me to start this work and helped with formatting the text and pictures.

Carol Rigby, who edited and proofread the manuscript.

PICTURE CREDITS

Picture of bombed house in "Chapter 1: Early Days," has no known copyright. The original photo is in the Egham Museum.

David Kilabuk Photography for the panorama of Pangnirtung.

The photograph of me and Margaret in the frontmatter is by Scott Wight Photography, of Ontario, Canada.

Tara Angnakak for illustrated maps.

Our daughter Susan for Matchbox house picture in "Chapter 3: Kinngait" and our house picture in "Chapter 5: Our Iqaluit Life."

The Diocese of the Arctic for the picture of the new Iqaluit Cathedral exterior.

Carol Rigby for scanned illustration of *Book of Common Prayer ... Translated into the Eastern Arctic Eskimo Tongue* published by the Diocese of the Arctic, Anglican Church of Canada, Rev. Ed. 1972.

All other photos are from my own personal family collection.

Manufactured by Amazon.ca
Bolton, ON